AF426296

Existential Reflections: Analyzing Sartre's No Exit and Nausea

Jean Francois Enrique

Published by Am I Am, 2024.

While every precaution has been taken in the preparation of this book, the publisher assumes no responsibility for errors or omissions, or for damages resulting from the use of the information contained herein.

EXISTENTIAL REFLECTIONS: ANALYZING SARTRE'S NO EXIT AND NAUSEA

First edition. August 1, 2024.

ISBN: 979-8227136107

Written by Jean Francois Enrique.

Existential Reflections: Analyzing Sartre's No Exit and Nausea

Dive deep into the world of existential philosophy with "Existential Reflections: Analyzing Sartre's 'No Exit' and 'Nausea.'" This comprehensive guide unpacks the profound themes and intricate ideas of Jean-Paul Sartre's most influential works. Explore the harrowing depths of human freedom, responsibility, and despair as Sartre envisioned them. Through detailed analysis and insightful commentary, this book offers readers a richer understanding of Sartre's existentialist perspective, making it an essential read for students, scholars, and anyone fascinated by the human condition. Unlock the existential truths of "No Exit" and "Nausea" and discover how Sartre's ideas continue to resonate in today's world.

EXISTENTIAL REFLECTIONS: Sartre's No Exit and Nausea
BY JEAN FRANCOIS ENRIQUE

TABLE OF CONTENTS

TABLE OF CONTENTS

SECTION ONE: SARTREAN EXISTENTIALISM

SECTION TWO: FOUNDATIONS OF EXISTENTIAL PHILOSOPHY

SECTION THREE: ANALYSIS OF NO EXIT

SECTION FOUR: ANALYSIS OF NAUSEA

SECTION FIVE: COMPARATIVE ANALYSIS

SECTION SIX: SARTRE'S PHILOSOPHICAL LEGACY

SECTION ONE: SARTREAN EXISTENTIALISM

1. UNDERSTANDING EXISTENTIALISM: THE PHILOSOPHY OF EXISTENCE

Existentialism, as a philosophical movement, emphasizes individual existence, freedom, and choice. It posits that individuals are free and responsible agents determining their own development through acts of the will. This philosophy arose as a response to the disorientation and confusion following the Great Wars and the rise of modernity, providing a framework for understanding human existence in an indifferent and often irrational universe.

Historically, existentialism emerged in the early 20th century, gaining prominence through the works of European philosophers such as Søren Kierkegaard, Friedrich Nietzsche, Martin Heidegger, and Jean-Paul Sartre. Though these thinkers varied in their approaches and conclusions, they shared a common concern with the human condition and the quest for meaning in a seemingly meaningless world. Their ideas were rooted in the turbulent socio-political context of their times, addressing the profound sense of alienation and loss of certainty that characterized the modern age.

At its core, existentialism is based on several key tenets. One of the foundational principles is the notion that "existence precedes essence." This idea, famously articulated by Jean-Paul Sartre, suggests that humans first exist without any predetermined purpose or essence and only later define themselves through their actions and choices. Unlike objects or tools, which are created with a specific function or essence in mind, humans must create their own meaning and purpose through their lived experiences.

Central to this process of self-definition is the concept of freedom and responsibility. Existentialist thought asserts that humans are radically free to make their own choices, but with this freedom comes the burden of responsibility for those choices. This freedom is not merely a matter of external circumstances but is intrinsic to human existence. Individuals must confront the anxiety and anguish that arise from their awareness of this freedom and the weight of their responsibilities.

Another crucial element of existentialism is the recognition of absurdity. The term "absurdity" in this context refers to the inherent lack of meaning in the universe and the human struggle to find or create meaning despite this. Existentialist philosophers argue that the universe is indifferent to human concerns, and any search for inherent meaning or order is ultimately futile. This confrontation with the absurd can lead to a sense of disillusionment, but it also offers an opportunity for individuals to assert their own values and create their own sense of purpose.

Authenticity and bad faith are also significant themes in existentialist philosophy. Authenticity involves living in accordance with one's true self and values, rather than conforming to external expectations or societal norms. It requires an honest acknowledgment of one's freedom and responsibility. In contrast, bad faith is a form of self-deception where individuals deny their freedom and responsibility by conforming to external pressures or hiding behind false identities. Living authentically means embracing one's freedom and making choices that reflect one's true nature and convictions.

Søren Kierkegaard, often regarded as the father of existentialism, introduced many of these ideas in the 19th century. His work focused on the individual's subjective experience and the leap of faith required to embrace religious belief in an uncertain world. Kierkegaard's emphasis on personal choice, commitment, and the struggle for authenticity laid the groundwork for later existentialist thought.

Friedrich Nietzsche, another pioneering figure, challenged traditional moral values and the notion of objective truth. He proclaimed the "death of God," suggesting that the decline of religious and metaphysical certainties left humanity in a state of existential crisis. Nietzsche advocated for the creation of new values and the embrace of life-affirming choices, encouraging individuals to live courageously and creatively in the face of nihilism.

Martin Heidegger's contributions to existentialism centered on the concept of "Being" and the human experience of existence. His magnum opus, "Being and Time," explored the nature of being, time, and human existence. Heidegger introduced the idea of "Being-toward-death," emphasizing the importance of confronting mortality and living authentically in light of the finite nature of human life.

Jean-Paul Sartre, perhaps the most famous existentialist, popularized and expanded upon these ideas in the mid-20th century. His works, such as "Being and Nothingness" and "Existentialism is a Humanism," articulated the fundamental principles of existentialism in accessible terms. Sartre emphasized the radical freedom and responsibility of individuals, the absurdity of existence, and the necessity of living authentically. He also explored the implications of existentialist thought for social and political engagement, advocating for a commitment to social justice and human rights.

In conclusion, existentialism is a rich and complex philosophical tradition that addresses the fundamental questions of human existence, freedom, and meaning. Its core ideas—existence preceding essence, the burden of freedom and responsibility, the recognition of absurdity, and the pursuit of authenticity—offer profound insights into the human condition. These concepts have not only shaped modern philosophy but have also had a significant impact on literature, psychology, and culture, influencing countless thinkers and artists.

The exploration of existentialism reveals a deep engagement with the challenges and possibilities of human existence, encouraging individuals to confront the realities of their freedom and to create their own meaning in a world that often seems indifferent or hostile. By embracing the principles of existentialism, one can navigate the complexities of life with greater self-awareness and a commitment to living authentically.

In the next article, we will delve deeper into the life and thought of Jean-Paul Sartre, examining his contributions to existentialism and his enduring influence on contemporary philosophy and culture. Sartre's work offers a compelling and nuanced understanding of existentialist thought, providing valuable insights into the nature of freedom, responsibility, and the quest for meaning in an ever-changing world.

2. JEAN-PAUL SARTRE: LIFE, INFLUENCE, AND PHILOSOPHY

Jean-Paul Sartre stands as one of the most influential figures in 20th-century philosophy, particularly known for his pivotal role in the development of existentialism. His philosophical explorations into human freedom, responsibility, and the search for meaning have left an indelible mark on contemporary thought. This article aims to provide an overview of Sartre's life, the profound influences that shaped his philosophy, and the lasting impact of his ideas.

Born on June 21, 1905, in Paris, Jean-Paul Charles Aymard Sartre was the only child of Jean-Baptiste Sartre, an officer in the French Navy, and Anne-Marie Schweitzer, cousin of the renowned humanitarian Albert Schweitzer. Sartre's father died when he was just fifteen months old, leaving him to be raised by his mother and her parents. This early loss instilled in Sartre a sense of independence and self-reliance that would characterize much of his later philosophical outlook.

Sartre's early education was marked by brilliance and rebellion. He attended the prestigious Lycée Henri-IV, where he developed a love for literature and philosophy. His academic journey continued at the École Normale Supérieure, one of France's leading institutions, where he formed lifelong friendships and intellectual alliances. It was here that Sartre first encountered the phenomenological ideas of Edmund Husserl and Martin Heidegger, which would significantly influence his own philosophical development.

A pivotal moment in Sartre's life came in 1929 when he met Simone de Beauvoir, a fellow philosophy student. Their relationship would become one of the most significant intellectual and personal partnerships of the 20th century. Beauvoir and Sartre challenged traditional notions of love and commitment, choosing to maintain an open relationship that allowed them both to pursue their individual passions and intellectual endeavors. This partnership not only shaped Sartre's personal life but also influenced his philosophical thinking, particularly his ideas on freedom and existentialism.

World War II was another defining period in Sartre's life. Conscripted into the French Army, he was captured by German forces in 1940 and spent nine months as a prisoner of war. This experience of captivity and his subsequent involvement in the French Resistance profoundly influenced his views on freedom, oppression, and human resilience.

Sartre's wartime experiences were reflected in his post-war writings, where he explored themes of existential anguish, the human condition, and the struggle for liberation.

Sartre's post-war years were marked by prolific writing and active engagement in political life. His existentialist masterpiece, "Being and Nothingness," published in 1943, laid the foundation for his philosophical legacy. In this work, Sartre elaborated on the concept of "being-for-itself," the idea that human existence is characterized by a constant striving to define oneself through actions and choices. He argued that individuals are condemned to be free, burdened with the responsibility of creating their own essence in a world devoid of inherent meaning.

The relationship with Simone de Beauvoir played a crucial role in Sartre's intellectual development. Together, they formed a dynamic duo, engaging in deep philosophical discussions and collaborations. Beauvoir's own work, particularly "The Second Sex," complemented Sartre's existentialist ideas by examining the oppression of women and the quest for authentic existence. Their partnership exemplified the intertwining of personal and philosophical life, demonstrating how intellectual and emotional bonds can shape one's worldview.

Sartre's experiences during World War II also had a profound impact on his philosophical outlook. Witnessing the horrors of war and the resilience of the human spirit, he became deeply committed to the idea of human freedom and the necessity of resisting oppression. His involvement in the French Resistance and his subsequent writings emphasized the importance of individual agency and the moral imperative to fight against tyranny. These experiences solidified Sartre's belief in the existentialist principle that humans are defined by their actions and choices.

In the post-war period, Sartre became increasingly involved in political activism, aligning himself with various leftist causes. He was a vocal critic of colonialism and supported anti-colonial movements in Algeria and Vietnam. Sartre's political engagement was reflected in his philosophical works, where he argued that true freedom could only be achieved through collective action and social justice. His play "Dirty Hands" and his essay "Colonialism and Neocolonialism" exemplify his commitment to these ideals, exploring the complexities of political struggle and the moral dilemmas faced by those involved in revolutionary movements.

Sartre's personal life and philosophical work were deeply interconnected, with his relationships, experiences, and political activism shaping his existentialist ideas. His partnership with Beauvoir, his wartime experiences, and his engagement in political struggles all contributed to his understanding of human existence, freedom, and responsibility. Sartre's life was a testament to the existentialist belief in the inseparability of thought and action, and his works continue to inspire and challenge readers to confront the fundamental questions of human existence.

In conclusion, Jean-Paul Sartre's life and philosophical journey were marked by a relentless quest to understand and articulate the complexities of human existence. His early experiences, profound personal relationships, and commitment to political activism all influenced his existentialist philosophy, which emphasized the freedom and responsibility of the individual in a world without inherent meaning. Sartre's legacy endures through his extensive body of work, which continues to provoke thought and inspire action.

In the next article, we will delve deeper into Sartre's major works, examining how his philosophical ideas were expressed in his literature and exploring the impact of his thought on contemporary philosophy and culture. Through a detailed analysis of texts such as "Being and Nothingness," "No Exit," and "Nausea," we will uncover the richness and depth of Sartre's existentialist vision and its enduring relevance in today's world.

3 THE SIGNIFICANCE OF SARTRE'S WORKS IN EXISTENTIAL PHILOSOPHY

Jean-Paul Sartre holds a pivotal place in the landscape of existential philosophy, largely due to his profound contributions through both his theoretical works and his literary creations. Sartre's exploration of human existence, freedom, and responsibility has shaped existentialist thought and left an enduring legacy in both philosophical circles and broader cultural contexts. His writings challenge readers to confront the deepest aspects of their own existence and the nature of the world around them. This article delves into the importance of Sartre's works within existential philosophy, providing an overview of his major works, key philosophical contributions, and their impact on literature and culture.

Sartre's magnum opus, "Being and Nothingness," published in 1943, stands as a cornerstone of existential philosophy. In this work, Sartre articulates his central thesis that "existence precedes essence," positing that human beings are not born with a predetermined nature or purpose. Instead, individuals must create their own essence through their actions and choices. This idea is foundational to existentialist thought, emphasizing the primacy of personal freedom and the responsibility that comes with it. "Being and Nothingness" introduces key concepts such as "being-for-itself" (human consciousness) and "being-in-itself" (the existence of objects), exploring the complex relationship between self-awareness and the external world. Sartre's rigorous analysis of these ideas provides a comprehensive framework for understanding the human condition and the challenges of existential freedom.

In "Existentialism is a Humanism," a lecture delivered in 1945 and later published, Sartre addresses common misconceptions about existentialism and clarifies its core principles. This work is particularly significant for its accessible presentation of existentialist ideas to a broader audience. Sartre argues that existentialism is an optimistic philosophy that empowers individuals to define their own lives and create meaning in an otherwise indifferent universe. He emphasizes the ethical dimension of existentialism, highlighting the responsibility individuals bear not only for their own actions but also for the impact those actions have on others. "Existentialism is a Humanism" thus serves as both a defense and a clarification of existentialist thought, reinforcing its relevance and importance.

"Nausea," Sartre's first novel published in 1938, explores existential themes through the experiences of its protagonist, Antoine Roquentin. The novel delves into the concept of "nausea" as a metaphor for the existential realization of the absurdity and contingency of existence. Roquentin's growing sense of alienation and his confrontation with the meaningless nature of the world around him encapsulate the existentialist struggle to find or create meaning in a chaotic and indifferent universe. "Nausea" poignantly captures the existential angst and despair that often accompany the recognition of one's absolute freedom and the burden of self-determination.

In his play "No Exit," written in 1944, Sartre presents a powerful dramatization of the existentialist concept that "hell is other people." The play features three characters trapped in a room for eternity, forced to confront the truths about themselves and each other. Through their interactions, Sartre explores the themes of self-deception, bad faith, and the inescapable gaze of the Other. "No Exit" underscores the idea that individuals are often defined and constrained by their relationships with others, highlighting the existential tension between self-definition and social existence.

Sartre's concept of existential freedom is a central contribution to existentialist philosophy. He posits that human beings are fundamentally free to make their own choices, unbound by any preordained essence or external determinism. This radical freedom is both a source of liberation and a profound burden, as individuals must take full responsibility for their actions and the course of their lives. Sartre's exploration of existential freedom challenges readers to acknowledge their autonomy and the ethical implications of their decisions.

The notion of bad faith, another key concept introduced by Sartre, refers to the act of self-deception in which individuals deny their own freedom and responsibility. Bad faith involves adopting false values or conforming to external pressures to avoid the anxiety associated with true freedom. By pretending to be something one is not, individuals escape the burden of authentic existence but also forsake their true potential. Sartre's analysis of bad faith illuminates the psychological mechanisms by which people evade the challenges of self-determination and the pursuit of authenticity.

Existential angst and despair are also central themes in Sartre's philosophy. These emotions arise from the realization of one's absolute freedom and the absence of inherent meaning in the universe. Sartre contends that while existential angst is an inevitable aspect of human existence, it also presents an opportunity for individuals to confront their freedom and create their own values. By embracing existential angst, individuals can achieve a deeper understanding of their own existence and the potential for authentic self-definition.

Sartre's influence extends beyond philosophy into existential psychoanalysis and Marxist existentialism. His collaboration with psychologist Maurice Merleau-Ponty and his engagement with Marxist theory enriched his existentialist framework, integrating insights from psychoanalysis and socio-political analysis. Sartre's existential psychoanalysis examines the ways in which individuals navigate their freedom and the psychological barriers to authentic existence. His Marxist existentialism, meanwhile, explores the intersection of existentialist thought with socio-political structures, emphasizing the importance of collective action and social justice in the pursuit of genuine freedom.

Sartre's role in the existentialist movement cannot be overstated. As a leading figure in the post-war existentialist community, Sartre's works inspired a generation of thinkers, writers, and artists. His ideas resonated deeply in a world grappling with the aftermath of war, the threat of totalitarianism, and the challenges of modernity. Sartre's existentialism provided a philosophical foundation for addressing the disorientation and alienation of the times, offering a path toward self-awareness and ethical engagement.

The impact of Sartre's thought on post-war literature and theater is significant. His existential themes influenced a wide range of writers and playwrights, from Albert Camus and Samuel Beckett to Harold Pinter and John-Paul Sartre. The exploration of existential angst, freedom, and authenticity in literature and theater reflects the profound influence of Sartre's philosophy on cultural expressions of the human condition. His works continue to inspire contemporary writers and artists, shaping the ways in which existential themes are explored and represented.

In contemporary philosophical thought, Sartre's legacy endures through ongoing discussions and debates about existentialism, freedom, and the nature of human existence. His contributions to existentialist philosophy remain relevant in addressing the existential challenges of the modern world, from the search for meaning in an increasingly fragmented society to the ethical implications of human freedom in a globalized context. Sartre's ideas continue to inspire new generations of philosophers, thinkers, and students, ensuring the enduring significance of his work.

In conclusion, Jean-Paul Sartre's works are of paramount importance in existential philosophy for their profound exploration of human existence, freedom, and responsibility. Through major works such as "Being and Nothingness," "Existentialism is a Humanism," "Nausea," and "No Exit," Sartre articulated key existentialist concepts and challenged readers to confront the deepest aspects of their own existence. His contributions to existential philosophy, his influence on literature and culture, and his engagement with existential psychoanalysis and Marxist existentialism underscore the enduring relevance of his ideas. Studying Sartre's works is essential for understanding the foundations of existentialist thought and its continued impact on contemporary philosophical and cultural discourse. Sartre's legacy remains a vital part of the philosophical exploration of the human condition, offering insights and challenges that continue to resonate in today's world.

SECTION TWO: FOUNDATIONS OF EXISTENTIAL PHILOSOPHY

4. ORIGINS AND KEY CONCEPTS: INTRODUCTION TO EXISTENTIALISM

Existentialism is a philosophical movement that emerged in the late 19th and early 20th centuries, emphasizing individual freedom, choice, and subjective experience. At its core, existential philosophy grapples with questions of human existence, the search for meaning, and the inherent absurdity of life. The movement rejects the notion that human beings are defined by pre-existing categories or essences, instead positing that individuals are free to create their own essence through actions and choices. This emphasis on individual freedom and responsibility has made existentialism both a deeply personal and profoundly influential philosophical tradition.

The origins of existentialism can be traced back to the works of several key thinkers who laid the groundwork for its development. Among the earliest of these were Søren Kierkegaard and Friedrich Nietzsche, whose writings in the 19th century introduced many of the themes and concepts that would later be central to existential thought. Kierkegaard, often considered the father of existentialism, focused on the individual's subjective experience and the challenges of living authentically in a world of uncertainty and despair. Nietzsche, on the other hand, challenged traditional moral values and emphasized the creative power of the individual in shaping their destiny.

Søren Kierkegaard (1813-1855) was a Danish philosopher and theologian whose work explored the complexities of faith, existence, and individuality. Kierkegaard's life was marked by a series of personal struggles and existential crises, which profoundly influenced his philosophical outlook. He believed that true understanding and meaning could only be found through personal experience and subjective reflection, rather than through rational analysis or objective knowledge. Kierkegaard's key concepts include the leap of faith, the individual, and subjectivity.

The leap of faith is one of Kierkegaard's most famous ideas, encapsulating the notion that belief in God or the acceptance of a meaningful existence requires a personal, non-rational commitment. According to Kierkegaard, this leap is necessary because objective certainty is unattainable in matters of faith and existential significance. Instead, individuals must confront the "absurd"—the paradoxes and uncertainties of life—and make a passionate, subjective choice to believe in something greater than themselves.

Kierkegaard also emphasized the importance of the individual in existential philosophy. He argued that each person is unique and must navigate their own path to authenticity and self-realization. This focus on individuality stands in contrast to the prevailing philosophical trends of his time, which often prioritized abstract concepts and universal truths over personal experience.

Subjectivity, for Kierkegaard, is the foundation of human existence. He believed that objective knowledge and rational thought could not capture the fullness of human life, which is characterized by emotions, passions, and personal commitments. By embracing subjectivity, individuals can engage with the deeper aspects of their existence and make meaningful choices that reflect their true selves.

Friedrich Nietzsche (1844-1900) was a German philosopher whose radical ideas challenged conventional moral and philosophical beliefs. Nietzsche's life was marked by a constant struggle against illness and adversity, which fueled his fierce critique of traditional values and his exploration of the potential for human greatness. Nietzsche's key concepts include the will to power, the eternal recurrence, and the Übermensch.

The will to power is a central idea in Nietzsche's philosophy, representing the fundamental driving force behind human actions and aspirations. Nietzsche believed that life is characterized by a constant striving for power, not necessarily in a political or physical sense, but as a manifestation of the individual's desire to assert their will and achieve their potential. This concept challenges the conventional understanding of morality and suggests that individuals should embrace their instincts and creativity to shape their own destiny.

The eternal recurrence is another profound idea introduced by Nietzsche, positing that all events in life will repeat infinitely in a cyclical pattern. This thought experiment forces individuals to confront the significance of their actions and the value of their lives. By imagining the eternal recurrence, Nietzsche encourages people to live authentically and passionately, as if every moment would recur eternally.

The Übermensch, or "overman," is Nietzsche's vision of an ideal human being who transcends conventional morality and creates their own values. The Übermensch represents the pinnacle of human potential, embodying creativity, strength, and self-mastery. Nietzsche's concept of the Übermensch challenges individuals to overcome their limitations and strive for greatness, rejecting the constraints of traditional morality and societal norms.

Martin Heidegger (1889-1976) was a German philosopher whose work profoundly influenced existentialism and contemporary philosophy. Heidegger's early life and academic career were deeply intertwined with the political turmoil of 20th-century Germany, and his complex relationship with National Socialism remains a subject of controversy. Nevertheless, Heidegger's contributions to existential philosophy are significant, particularly through his exploration of the nature of Being and human existence.

Heidegger's magnum opus, "Being and Time," introduces the concept of Dasein, which refers to the unique way in which human beings exist in the world. Dasein, or "being-there," captures the essence of human existence as fundamentally temporal, situated, and engaged with the world. Heidegger argues that traditional metaphysics has overlooked the question of Being, and he seeks to uncover the fundamental structures of existence through a phenomenological analysis of Dasein.

Central to Heidegger's philosophy is the question of Being, which he believes is the most fundamental and overlooked question in Western philosophy. Heidegger's investigation into Being involves examining the ways in which humans relate to the world and to their own existence. He introduces the concept of "thrownness" (Geworfenheit) to describe the condition of being thrown into a pre-existing world with specific contexts and limitations. This idea underscores the inherent constraints and possibilities of human existence.

Heidegger also explores the concept of "authenticity," which involves confronting the realities of existence, including the inevitability of death, and making choices that reflect one's true self. Authenticity requires a recognition of the finite nature of life and a commitment to living in a way that is true to one's own values and aspirations, rather than conforming to external pressures or societal expectations.

Core themes in existential philosophy revolve around the exploration of human freedom and choice, the search for meaning, and the confrontation with absurdity. Existentialism asserts that individuals are fundamentally free to make their own choices and create their own meaning, despite the inherent uncertainties and challenges of life. This emphasis on freedom and responsibility distinguishes existentialism from other philosophical traditions that emphasize determinism or objective truths.

Human freedom and choice are central to existential thought. Existential philosophers argue that individuals are not bound by predetermined essences or external authorities; instead, they are free to shape their own destinies through their actions and decisions. This freedom, however, is accompanied by a profound sense of responsibility, as individuals must navigate the consequences of their choices and confront the inherent uncertainties of life.

The search for meaning is another core theme in existential philosophy. Existentialists contend that life does not come with inherent meaning or purpose; rather, individuals must create their own meaning through their experiences, relationships, and commitments. This search for meaning often involves grappling with the absurdity of existence—the recognition that life can be irrational, chaotic, and devoid of inherent purpose.

The confrontation with absurdity is a defining aspect of existential thought. The absurd arises from the tension between the human desire for meaning and the indifferent, often irrational nature of the universe. Existential philosophers like Kierkegaard, Nietzsche, and Heidegger explore how individuals can confront this absurdity and find ways to live authentically and meaningfully despite the inherent challenges.

Existentialism also emphasizes the importance of individual existence and authenticity. Existentialists argue that each person's existence is unique and cannot be fully understood through abstract concepts or universal truths. Authenticity involves embracing one's individuality and making choices that reflect one's true self, rather than conforming to external pressures or societal norms.

In conclusion, existentialism is a rich and multifaceted philosophical tradition that addresses some of the most profound questions of human existence. Through the contributions of key thinkers like Søren Kierkegaard, Friedrich Nietzsche, and Martin Heidegger, existentialism explores themes of freedom, choice, meaning, and absurdity, emphasizing the importance of individual experience and authenticity. This philosophical movement continues to resonate with contemporary audiences, offering insights into the complexities of human life and the possibilities for personal growth and self-realization.

5. LIFE AND INFLUENCE

Jean-Paul Sartre was a towering figure in 20th-century philosophy, literature, and political thought, known for his profound contributions to existentialism. Born in Paris on June 21, 1905, Sartre's intellectual journey began early. He studied at the École Normale Supérieure, where he was deeply influenced by the ideas of German phenomenology, particularly the works of Edmund Husserl and Martin Heidegger. Sartre's intellectual background was diverse, encompassing philosophy, literature, and psychology, which allowed him to approach existentialism from a unique and multifaceted perspective.

During World War II, Sartre was conscripted into the French army and subsequently captured by German forces. His time as a prisoner of war had a profound impact on his thinking, particularly regarding the nature of human freedom and responsibility. After his release, Sartre became actively involved in the French Resistance, using his writings to oppose Nazi occupation and promote the ideals of freedom and human dignity. This period was crucial in shaping his post-war existentialist philosophy, as he grappled with the realities of oppression, resistance, and the moral complexities of human action.

Sartre's role in the French Resistance and his subsequent influence on post-war existentialism cannot be overstated. His experiences during the war solidified his belief in the importance of human freedom and the necessity of individual responsibility in the face of societal and political constraints. After the war, Sartre became one of the leading intellectuals in France, promoting existentialist ideas through his prolific writing and public lectures. His work resonated deeply with a generation recovering from the horrors of war, offering a framework for understanding the human condition and the challenges of living authentically in a complex and often absurd world.

One of Sartre's most significant contributions to existentialism is his exploration of human freedom. For Sartre, freedom is the defining characteristic of human existence. He famously articulated this idea with the phrase "existence precedes essence," meaning that humans are not born with a predetermined nature or purpose; instead, they must create their own essence through their actions and choices. This concept stands in stark contrast to traditional philosophical and religious views that posit a fixed human nature or divine plan.

Sartre's view on human freedom is both liberating and daunting. On one hand, it empowers individuals to shape their own destinies and live authentically according to their values and aspirations. On the other hand, it imposes a heavy burden of responsibility, as individuals must constantly navigate the consequences of their choices without the comfort of predetermined guidelines. This radical freedom, Sartre argues, is the source of both human dignity and existential anxiety.

A central theme in Sartre's existentialism is the concept of bad faith (mauvaise foi). Bad faith refers to the act of denying one's own freedom and responsibility by adopting false values or conforming to external pressures. It is a form of self-deception in which individuals hide from the inherent uncertainties and responsibilities of existence by pretending that they are bound by fixed roles or societal norms. For example, a person might claim that they have no choice but to follow a certain career path because of family expectations, thereby avoiding the anxiety of making a truly free decision.

Bad faith manifests in everyday life in numerous ways. It can be seen in the rigid adherence to social roles, the evasion of personal responsibility, and the denial of one's own desires and potential. Sartre argues that bad faith is a universal human tendency, as the weight of freedom and the fear of making wrong choices often lead individuals to seek refuge in self-deception. However, he also believes that it is possible to overcome bad faith by embracing authenticity, which involves acknowledging one's freedom and taking full responsibility for one's actions.

The absurd is another key concept in Sartre's existentialism. The absurd arises from the conflict between the human desire for meaning and the indifferent, often chaotic nature of the universe. Sartre's interpretation of the absurd builds on the ideas of earlier existentialists like Albert Camus, emphasizing the inherent lack of meaning in the world and the individual's struggle to create meaning in the face of this void. The absurdity of existence challenges individuals to confront the irrationality and unpredictability of life and to find ways to live meaningfully despite these challenges.

In Sartre's view, the relationship between absurdity and human existence is complex and multifaceted. On one hand, the recognition of the absurd can lead to feelings of despair and nihilism, as individuals grapple with the apparent meaninglessness of life. On the other hand, it can also be a source of liberation, as it frees individuals from the illusion of predetermined purpose and allows them to create their own meaning through their choices and actions. Sartre encourages individuals to embrace the absurd and to live authentically by accepting the uncertainty of existence and committing to their own values and goals.

Sartre's major works, particularly "Being and Nothingness" and "Existentialism is a Humanism," have had a profound impact on existential philosophy and contemporary thought. "Being and Nothingness," published in 1943, is Sartre's seminal philosophical work, offering a comprehensive exploration of his existentialist ideas. The book delves into the nature of consciousness, freedom, and the self, arguing that human existence is characterized by a fundamental nothingness or lack of essence that allows for radical freedom. Sartre also examines the dynamics of interpersonal relationships, introducing concepts such as "the look" and "being-for-others," which explore how individuals perceive and are perceived by others.

A particularly famous concept from "Being and Nothingness" is Sartre's assertion that "Hell is other people" ("L'enfer, c'est les autres"). This idea is explored in his play "No Exit," where three characters are confined together in a room for eternity. The phrase highlights the existentialist view that the presence and judgment of others can be a source of profound anxiety and self-alienation. Sartre illustrates how individuals often allow their sense of self to be shaped by the perceptions and expectations of others, leading to a loss of authenticity and freedom. This dynamic creates a metaphorical "hell" in which individuals are trapped by the gaze and judgments of those around them, unable to achieve true self-realization.

"Being and Nothingness" is a dense and challenging text, but its influence on existential and contemporary philosophy is immense. It provides a rigorous theoretical foundation for Sartre's ideas, offering a detailed analysis of the structures of human existence and the implications of existential freedom. The book has inspired countless philosophers, writers, and thinkers, shaping discussions on topics ranging from phenomenology and ontology to ethics and psychology.

"Existentialism is a Humanism," a public lecture delivered by Sartre in 1945, serves as a more accessible introduction to his existentialist philosophy. In this lecture, Sartre defends existentialism against common criticisms, arguing that it is a philosophy of action and human dignity. He asserts that existentialism is not a form of nihilism, but rather a call to embrace the freedom and responsibility inherent in human existence. By rejecting the notion of predetermined essence and emphasizing the importance of individual choice, Sartre presents existentialism as a philosophy that empowers individuals to live authentically and meaningfully.

The significance of "Existentialism is a Humanism" lies in its clear and concise articulation of Sartre's key ideas, making existentialist thought accessible to a broader audience. The lecture has become one of Sartre's most famous and widely read works, offering a compelling defense of existentialism and its relevance to modern life.

Sartre's legacy extends far beyond his philosophical writings. His influence on later existentialist thinkers and movements is profound, shaping the development of existential psychology, literature, and political thought. Sartre's emphasis on human freedom, authenticity, and responsibility has resonated with generations of thinkers, inspiring new approaches to understanding the human condition and addressing the challenges of modern life.

In literature, Sartre's existentialist themes have been explored and expanded upon by writers such as Albert Camus, Simone de Beauvoir, and Samuel Beckett. These authors have used fiction to delve into the complexities of existential freedom, the absurd, and the search for meaning, creating works that continue to captivate and challenge readers.

Sartre's impact on theatre is also significant, particularly through his plays such as "No Exit" and "The Flies." These works dramatize existential themes, using the stage to explore the dynamics of freedom, choice, and bad faith. Sartre's influence on modern drama is evident in the works of playwrights like Harold Pinter and Tom Stoppard, who have similarly grappled with existential questions in their plays.

In the realm of political thought, Sartre's existentialism has informed various movements and ideologies, from existential Marxism to existential feminism. His commitment to social justice and human dignity has inspired activists and theorists to address issues of oppression, freedom, and ethical responsibility in their work. Sartre's involvement in political activism, particularly his support for anti-colonial struggles and his critique of bourgeois society, has also left a lasting mark on political discourse.

In conclusion, Jean-Paul Sartre's contributions to existentialism are vast and enduring. Through his exploration of human freedom, bad faith, and the absurd, Sartre has provided a framework for understanding the complexities of human existence and the challenges of living authentically. His major works, "Being and Nothingness" and "Existentialism is a Humanism," have had a profound impact on existential philosophy and contemporary thought, inspiring generations of thinkers and writers. Sartre's legacy extends beyond philosophy, influencing literature, theatre, and political thought, and his ideas continue to resonate with those seeking to navigate the uncertainties and possibilities of modern life.

6. EXISTENTIAL THEMES IN LITERATURE AND ART

Existential themes in literature and art have played a significant role in shaping 20th-century culture. This exploration delves into the complex and often unsettling questions of human existence, freedom, meaning, and the absurd. Existentialism, as a philosophical movement, found a fertile ground in the creative expressions of novels, plays, and visual art, where its ideas were not only illustrated but also expanded and deepened. Three key figures who significantly contributed to this cultural phenomenon are Albert Camus, Franz Kafka, and Samuel Beckett. Their works have profoundly influenced how existential ideas are understood and appreciated, transcending philosophical discourse to resonate deeply with the broader public.

In literature, Albert Camus stands out as a central figure in existential thought, though he often resisted being labeled as an existentialist. Camus' novels, such as "The Stranger," "The Plague," and "The Fall," encapsulate his exploration of the absurd and the human struggle for meaning in an indifferent universe. "The Stranger" introduces readers to Meursault, a detached and dispassionate character who confronts the absurdity of life following the death of his mother and his subsequent murder of an Arab man. Meursault's existential awakening occurs in his recognition of the universe's indifference and the realization that human life is devoid of inherent meaning. This novel exemplifies Camus' belief in the absurd: the conflict between humans' desire for significance and the silent, indifferent world.

"The Plague," another seminal work by Camus, serves as an allegory for the human condition and the absurdity of suffering. Set in the Algerian city of Oran, which is struck by a deadly plague, the novel follows various characters' responses to the crisis. Through Dr. Rieux and others, Camus explores themes of solidarity, resistance, and the search for meaning amidst the apparent senselessness of suffering. The plague becomes a metaphor for the human condition, where individuals must confront the reality of death and find ways to live meaningfully despite the inevitability of suffering and loss.

Franz Kafka's works, though predating the formal existentialist movement, are often considered quintessential explorations of existential themes. Kafka's novels and short stories, such as "The Trial," "The Metamorphosis," and "The Castle," delve into the nightmarish, often surreal experiences of individuals confronting an incomprehensible and indifferent world. "The Trial" tells the story of Josef K., a man inexplicably arrested and prosecuted by a distant, opaque authority. The novel captures the essence of existential dread and the absurdity of seeking justice or meaning in a world governed by arbitrary and unfathomable forces.

"The Metamorphosis," perhaps Kafka's most famous work, presents the bizarre transformation of Gregor Samsa into a gigantic insect. This surreal event plunges Gregor into a profound existential crisis, as he grapples with his altered identity, his estrangement from his family, and his increasing isolation. Kafka's exploration of alienation, guilt, and the search for meaning in an absurd existence resonates deeply with existentialist themes, highlighting the individual's struggle to find coherence and purpose in a fragmented and often hostile world.

Samuel Beckett's contribution to existential literature and drama is monumental, particularly through his play "Waiting for Godot." Beckett's minimalist and often bleak style reflects the core existentialist idea of the absurd. "Waiting for Godot" features two characters, Vladimir and Estragon, who wait endlessly and in vain for the arrival of someone named Godot. The play's sparse setting and repetitive dialogue underscore the futility and meaninglessness of their wait, mirroring the existential belief that life is an endless search for meaning in an indifferent universe.

Beckett's work extends beyond "Waiting for Godot" to other plays and novels that further explore existential themes. His novel "Molloy," part of the trilogy that includes "Malone Dies" and "The Unnamable," delves into the fragmented consciousness and the existential plight of its protagonists. Beckett's characters often face an existence stripped of purpose, where language and thought fail to provide clarity or solace. Through his exploration of the limits of communication and the inherent isolation of the human condition, Beckett captures the existential struggle for meaning and the pervasive sense of absurdity.

Existential themes in visual art during the 20th century were also prominent, reflecting the angst and disillusionment of the era. The existential crisis induced by the two World Wars, the threat of nuclear annihilation, and the rapid technological and social changes found expression in various art movements and individual works. Abstract Expressionism, for instance, emerged in the post-war period as a response to the existential anxieties of the time. Artists like Jackson Pollock, Mark Rothko, and Willem de Kooning used abstraction to convey the tumultuous inner states and the search for meaning in a chaotic world.

Pollock's technique of "drip painting," where he would pour and splatter paint onto a canvas laid on the ground, reflects a kind of existential freedom and spontaneity. His works, devoid of clear structure or form, invite viewers to confront the chaos and unpredictability of existence. Rothko's large, color-field paintings, with their luminous, floating rectangles, evoke a sense of profound stillness and contemplation. Rothko aimed to express fundamental human emotions and the spiritual search for meaning, making his works resonant with existentialist themes.

Similarly, the Surrealist movement, with artists like Salvador Dalí, René Magritte, and Max Ernst, delved into the unconscious and the irrational aspects of the human experience. Surrealist art often depicted dream-like, fantastical scenes that challenged conventional reality, reflecting the existentialist idea of questioning the nature of existence and the boundaries of reality. Dalí's "The Persistence of Memory," with its melting clocks and eerie landscape, symbolizes the fluidity and elusiveness of time and reality, echoing existential concerns about the nature of existence and the human condition.

In literature and art, existential themes have profoundly shaped 20th-century culture, reflecting the period's disillusionment, anxiety, and the search for meaning. The works of Albert Camus, Franz Kafka, and Samuel Beckett, among others, have provided rich and nuanced explorations of existentialist ideas, influencing countless writers, artists, and thinkers. Camus' novels confront the absurd and the human struggle for meaning, Kafka's stories delve into the alienation and incomprehensibility of the modern world, and Beckett's plays and novels highlight the futility and repetitive nature of human existence.

These existential explorations were not limited to literature alone. In visual art, movements like Abstract Expressionism and Surrealism provided powerful expressions of existential themes. Artists like Jackson Pollock and Mark Rothko used abstraction to convey the chaos and search for meaning in post-war society, while Surrealists like Salvador Dalí and René Magritte explored the irrational and dream-like dimensions of existence.

The impact of existentialism on 20th-century culture is evident in how these themes have permeated various forms of creative expression. Literature and art became mediums through which the complexities of human existence, freedom, and the search for meaning could be examined and articulated. Existentialist ideas challenged individuals to confront the uncertainties and absurdities of life, inspiring a deeper reflection on the nature of existence and the human condition.

In addition to the works of Camus, Kafka, and Beckett, other writers and artists also contributed to the existentialist dialogue. For instance, Jean-Paul Sartre's plays, such as "No Exit" and "The Flies," further explored themes of freedom, responsibility, and bad faith. Sartre's assertion that "Hell is other people" encapsulates the existentialist tension between individual freedom and the often oppressive nature of social relationships.

The existentialist influence extended to the Beat Generation in American literature, with writers like Jack Kerouac and Allen Ginsberg exploring themes of alienation, freedom, and the search for authenticity. Kerouac's "On the Road" and Ginsberg's "Howl" reflect the existentialist quest for meaning and the rejection of conventional societal norms.

In the visual arts, the existentialist ethos was reflected in the work of post-war European artists like Alberto Giacometti and Francis Bacon. Giacometti's elongated, emaciated sculptures evoke a sense of existential isolation and the fragility of human existence, while Bacon's grotesque, distorted figures capture the angst and turmoil of the human condition.

Overall, the exploration of existential themes in literature and art has left an indelible mark on 20th-century culture. Through the works of key figures like Albert Camus, Franz Kafka, and Samuel Beckett, and the broader artistic movements they influenced, existentialism has provided a framework for understanding the complexities of human existence. By grappling with questions of freedom, meaning, and the absurd, these creative expressions have offered profound insights into the human condition, resonating with audiences and shaping the cultural landscape of the modern era.

7. EXISTENTIALISM AND RELIGION

Existentialism and religion have a complex and multifaceted relationship, with existential philosophy providing a unique lens through which to explore questions of faith, doubt, and the meaning of life. While existentialism often grapples with themes traditionally addressed by religion—such as the search for meaning, the confrontation with death, and the nature of human existence—it approaches these questions from a standpoint that emphasizes individual experience and subjective interpretation. The tension and dialogue between existentialism and religious thought are particularly evident when examining the works of both atheist existentialists, such as Jean-Paul Sartre and Albert Camus, and theistic existentialists, such as Søren Kierkegaard and Gabriel Marcel.

Atheist existentialists like Sartre and Camus approach existential questions from a perspective that denies the existence of a divine or transcendent being. For Sartre, the absence of God is a fundamental premise of his existential philosophy. He famously asserted that "existence precedes essence," meaning that humans are not born with a predetermined purpose or essence given by a creator. Instead, individuals must create their own essence through their choices and actions. This perspective leads to a radical form of freedom, where each person is entirely responsible for giving their life meaning in a universe that is indifferent to human existence.

Sartre's atheistic existentialism is deeply rooted in the concept of freedom and the burden of responsibility that accompanies it. Without a divine authority to provide moral guidance or an ultimate purpose, individuals are left to navigate their own paths, making choices that define their essence. This freedom, while empowering, also brings with it a profound sense of existential angst, as individuals must confront the inherent meaninglessness of life and the weight of their own decisions.

Albert Camus, another prominent atheist existentialist, also grapples with the implications of a godless universe. In his philosophical essay "The Myth of Sisyphus," Camus explores the idea of the absurd—the conflict between the human desire for meaning and the silent, indifferent world. Camus argues that the recognition of the absurd is a fundamental aspect of the human condition, but rather than leading to despair, it can inspire a form of defiant joy. By embracing the absurd and continuing to search for meaning despite its elusiveness, individuals can find a sense of freedom and authenticity.

Camus' novels, such as "The Stranger" and "The Plague," further illustrate his existential themes. "The Stranger" follows the protagonist Meursault, who embodies the existential hero by living in the moment and rejecting societal conventions. His indifference to traditional moral values and his acceptance of the absurdity of life challenge readers to reconsider the foundations of meaning and morality in a world without God.

In contrast to the atheistic existentialists, theistic existentialists like Søren Kierkegaard and Gabriel Marcel approach existential questions within the framework of religious faith. Kierkegaard, often considered the father of existentialism, was deeply religious and his writings reflect a profound engagement with Christian theology. Kierkegaard's existentialism is centered on the individual's relationship with God and the personal, subjective nature of faith.

Kierkegaard's concept of the "leap of faith" is a cornerstone of his existential thought. He argued that true faith is not a matter of rational certainty but a passionate, subjective commitment to belief in the face of doubt and uncertainty. This leap of faith requires individuals to confront the absurdity and paradoxes of existence and make a personal commitment to God that transcends rational understanding. For Kierkegaard, this subjective approach to faith is essential to living an authentic and meaningful life.

Gabriel Marcel, another theistic existentialist, also emphasized the importance of faith and the transcendent. Marcel's existentialism is deeply relational, focusing on the connections between individuals and the presence of the divine in everyday life. He viewed human existence as fundamentally mysterious and argued that this mystery could only be fully understood through a relationship with the transcendent. Marcel's philosophy emphasizes hope, love, and fidelity as central to the human experience, and he saw religious faith as a means of engaging with the deeper mysteries of existence.

The contrast between atheist and theistic existentialists highlights different approaches to existential questions, particularly regarding the nature of faith, doubt, and the meaning of life. While atheist existentialists like Sartre and Camus reject the notion of a divine or transcendent being and emphasize human freedom and responsibility in a godless universe, theistic existentialists like Kierkegaard and Marcel find meaning through a personal relationship with God and the embrace of religious faith.

Both approaches, however, share a common emphasis on the individual's experience and the importance of personal authenticity. Existentialists, whether atheist or theistic, reject the idea that meaning and purpose can be imposed from external sources or predefined categories. Instead, they argue that individuals must actively engage with their own existence, confront the challenges and uncertainties of life, and create their own meaning through their choices and commitments.

Existential approaches to faith and doubt are deeply intertwined with the broader existential themes of freedom, responsibility, and authenticity. For atheist existentialists, the absence of God means that individuals must confront the absurdity of existence and find ways to live meaningfully despite the lack of inherent purpose. This often involves a rejection of traditional moral and religious frameworks and a focus on personal freedom and self-creation.

For example, Sartre's concept of "bad faith" involves the denial of one's own freedom and responsibility by conforming to external pressures or adopting false values. Living authentically, for Sartre, means acknowledging the reality of one's freedom and taking full responsibility for one's actions, even in the face of existential anxiety and the apparent meaninglessness of life. This perspective challenges individuals to create their own meaning and live according to their own values, rather than seeking solace in predetermined roles or societal norms.

Camus' approach to faith and doubt is similarly rooted in the recognition of the absurd. While he rejects traditional religious faith, he advocates for a form of existential rebellion against the absurdity of existence. By embracing the absurd and continuing to search for meaning despite its elusiveness, individuals can find a sense of freedom and authenticity. This defiance in the face of the absurd is exemplified in the figure of Sisyphus, who, despite the futility of his task, continues to push the boulder up the hill with a sense of purpose and determination.

In contrast, theistic existentialists like Kierkegaard and Marcel approach faith and doubt within the context of a relationship with the divine. Kierkegaard's concept of the leap of faith involves embracing the uncertainty and paradoxes of existence and making a personal, subjective commitment to God. This leap requires individuals to move beyond rational certainty and trust in the transcendent, finding meaning and purpose through their relationship with the divine.

Marcel's approach to faith emphasizes the relational and mysterious aspects of human existence. He argues that true understanding of the self and the world can only be achieved through a relationship with the transcendent, and that religious faith provides a means of engaging with the deeper mysteries of existence. For Marcel, hope, love, and fidelity are central to the human experience, and faith is an essential component of living authentically and meaningfully.

Despite their differences, both atheist and theistic existentialists offer valuable insights into the nature of faith, doubt, and the meaning of life. By emphasizing the individual's experience and the importance of personal authenticity, existentialism provides a framework for exploring these questions in a way that is deeply personal and relevant to contemporary concerns.

In summary, the relationship between existential philosophy and religious thought is characterized by a rich and nuanced dialogue that spans both atheist and theistic perspectives. Atheist existentialists like Sartre and Camus challenge traditional religious frameworks and emphasize human freedom and responsibility in a godless universe, while theistic existentialists like Kierkegaard and Marcel find meaning through a personal relationship with God and the embrace of religious faith. Both approaches share a common emphasis on the individual's experience and the importance of personal authenticity, offering profound insights into the nature of faith, doubt, and the search for meaning in the modern world. Through this exploration, existentialism continues to provide a valuable lens for understanding the complexities of human existence and the enduring questions of faith and meaning.

8. EXISTENTIALISM AND PSYCHOLOGY

Existentialism has had a profound influence on modern psychology and psychotherapy, providing a framework for understanding human experience that emphasizes individual freedom, choice, and the search for meaning. The existentialist perspective in psychology focuses on the human condition as it relates to themes such as existence, anxiety, death, isolation, and the pursuit of authenticity. This philosophical approach has significantly shaped the development of existential therapy, which seeks to address the fundamental issues of human existence and help individuals find meaning and purpose in their lives. Two key figures who have been instrumental in integrating existential thought into psychology are Viktor Frankl and Rollo May. Their contributions have laid the foundation for existential therapy and its applications in contemporary practice.

Viktor Frankl, an Austrian psychiatrist and Holocaust survivor, is best known for developing logotherapy, a form of existential analysis that emphasizes the search for meaning as the primary motivational force in human life. Frankl's experiences in Nazi concentration camps profoundly shaped his understanding of human resilience and the capacity to find meaning even in the most horrific circumstances. His seminal work, "Man's Search for Meaning," chronicles his observations and insights from his time in the camps, highlighting the importance of finding purpose as a means of enduring suffering.

Frankl's logotherapy is grounded in the existential belief that life has inherent meaning, and it is the individual's responsibility to discover and fulfill it. According to Frankl, meaning can be found in three primary ways: through work or creating something, through experiencing something or encountering someone, and through the attitude one adopts toward unavoidable suffering. He argued that even in situations where individuals have no control over their circumstances, they still have the freedom to choose their attitude and find meaning in their suffering. This perspective aligns with existentialist ideas about freedom and responsibility, emphasizing the power of personal choice in shaping one's existence.

Logotherapy has had a significant impact on the field of psychotherapy, offering a framework for helping individuals navigate existential crises and find purpose in their lives. In practice, logotherapy involves helping clients identify and pursue meaningful goals, reflect on their values, and develop a sense of purpose. It encourages individuals to transcend their immediate circumstances and connect with something greater than themselves, whether through creative endeavors, relationships, or a commitment to a cause. This focus on meaning and purpose can be particularly beneficial for individuals experiencing existential anxiety, depression, or feelings of emptiness and despair.

Rollo May, an American psychologist, is another pivotal figure in the integration of existential thought into psychology. May's work emphasized the existential themes of anxiety, freedom, and the search for authenticity. He was deeply influenced by the existential philosophy of Søren Kierkegaard and Friedrich Nietzsche, as well as the existential-phenomenological approach of Martin Heidegger. May's contributions to existential psychology are encapsulated in his influential books, such as "The Meaning of Anxiety" and "Love and Will."

May's existential psychology is centered on the idea that anxiety is an inevitable part of the human experience, arising from the awareness of our freedom and the responsibility that comes with it. He distinguished between normal anxiety, which is proportionate to the situation and can be a catalyst for growth, and neurotic anxiety, which is disproportionate and paralyzing. According to May, confronting and embracing normal anxiety is essential for personal development and self-actualization. By acknowledging our freedom and the uncertainties of existence, we can make authentic choices that reflect our true values and aspirations.

In his work, May also explored the concept of love and its role in human existence. He viewed love as a fundamental aspect of being that encompasses various forms, including eros (romantic love), philia (friendship), and agape (unconditional love). May believed that genuine love involves a deep respect for the other person's individuality and freedom, and it requires courage and commitment. This perspective on love is closely linked to existential ideas about authentic relationships and the importance of connecting with others while maintaining one's own autonomy.

Existential therapy, as developed by Frankl, May, and other existential thinkers, focuses on helping individuals confront and make sense of the fundamental issues of existence. Unlike traditional psychotherapies that may emphasize symptom reduction or behavioral change, existential therapy aims to address the deeper questions of meaning, purpose, and authenticity. It encourages clients to explore their values, reflect on their life choices, and develop a sense of responsibility for their own existence.

In contemporary practice, existential therapy is applied in various contexts and with diverse populations. It is particularly effective in addressing existential crises, such as those triggered by major life transitions, loss, or trauma. For example, individuals facing terminal illness or the loss of a loved one may benefit from existential therapy's focus on finding meaning in suffering and embracing the realities of mortality. By helping clients explore their existential concerns and develop a sense of purpose, existential therapists can facilitate a deeper understanding of the self and promote psychological resilience.

Existential therapy also plays a crucial role in addressing issues related to identity and authenticity. In a world where individuals are often pressured to conform to societal expectations or adopt inauthentic roles, existential therapy provides a space for clients to explore their true selves and make choices that align with their core values. This process of self-exploration and authenticity can lead to greater self-acceptance and fulfillment, as individuals learn to live in accordance with their own beliefs and aspirations rather than external standards.

Moreover, existential therapy's emphasis on the therapeutic relationship is a key component of its effectiveness. Existential therapists strive to create an authentic and empathetic connection with their clients, fostering a collaborative and non-judgmental environment. This relational approach is grounded in the belief that the therapist-client relationship itself can be a source of meaning and growth, as it allows clients to experience genuine human connection and develop a deeper understanding of themselves through the therapeutic process.

In addition to its applications in individual therapy, existential principles are also integrated into other therapeutic approaches and settings. For example, existential themes are often incorporated into humanistic therapies, such as person-centered therapy and gestalt therapy, which share a focus on personal growth, self-actualization, and the exploration of subjective experience. Existential ideas also inform group therapy and support groups, where individuals can share their existential concerns and learn from the experiences of others.

The influence of existential thought on psychology extends beyond therapy to broader discussions about mental health and well-being. Existential ideas challenge the reductionist and deterministic views often found in traditional psychology, advocating for a more holistic understanding of the human experience. By emphasizing the importance of meaning, choice, and authenticity, existential psychology encourages a more nuanced and compassionate approach to mental health that acknowledges the complexities of human existence.

Furthermore, existential psychology has contributed to the development of positive psychology, which focuses on the strengths and potential of individuals rather than solely on pathology. Concepts such as resilience, flourishing, and the pursuit of meaning are central to both existential and positive psychology, highlighting the importance of understanding and nurturing the positive aspects of human experience.

In conclusion, the influence of existential thought on modern psychology and psychotherapy has been profound and far-reaching. Through the pioneering work of figures like Viktor Frankl and Rollo May, existentialism has provided a rich framework for exploring the fundamental questions of human existence and addressing the deeper issues that underlie psychological distress. Existential therapy, with its focus on meaning, authenticity, and the therapeutic relationship, offers a powerful approach to helping individuals navigate the complexities of life and find purpose and fulfillment. By integrating existential principles into various therapeutic approaches and settings, modern psychology continues to benefit from the insights of existential philosophy, fostering a more holistic and compassionate understanding of mental health and well-being.

9. CRITIQUES AND CONTROVERSIES

Existentialism, as a philosophical movement, has been both influential and contentious since its inception. Originating in the 19th and 20th centuries with thinkers like Søren Kierkegaard, Friedrich Nietzsche, Jean-Paul Sartre, and Martin Heidegger, existentialism has provoked a wide array of critiques and controversies. These critiques come from various philosophical perspectives, highlighting fundamental disagreements about human nature, freedom, and the pursuit of meaning. Additionally, the movement has faced internal debates and misconceptions that have further complicated its reception and development. In the 21st century, existentialism continues to be relevant, but it also encounters new criticisms in the context of contemporary issues.

One of the major critiques of existentialism comes from the perspective of analytic philosophy. Analytic philosophers have often criticized existentialism for its perceived lack of rigor and clarity. Figures like A.J. Ayer and Bertrand Russell argued that existentialist texts are often obscure, overly metaphorical, and lacking in logical structure. This critique centers on the idea that existentialism, with its focus on subjective experience and existential angst, fails to meet the standards of philosophical precision and logical analysis that are valued in the analytic tradition. As a result, existentialism is sometimes dismissed as more literary or poetic than genuinely philosophical.

Another significant critique comes from the Marxist tradition. Marxist philosophers, such as Georg Lukács, have argued that existentialism is overly individualistic and fails to adequately address the social and economic conditions that shape human existence. From a Marxist perspective, existentialism's emphasis on individual freedom and personal responsibility can obscure the structural forces that constrain human agency. By focusing on existential anxiety and the individual's search for meaning, existentialism is seen as neglecting the material conditions of life and the collective struggle for social justice. This critique points to a fundamental tension between existentialism's emphasis on personal authenticity and the Marxist focus on class struggle and social change.

Existentialism has also been critiqued from a feminist perspective. Some feminist philosophers have argued that existentialism, particularly in the works of Sartre and Heidegger, tends to privilege a male-centered view of the human experience. Simone de Beauvoir, a key figure in both existentialism and feminism, critiqued this bias in her own work, "The Second Sex." She argued that existentialism often fails to account for the specific ways in which women experience existential issues, such as freedom and oppression. De Beauvoir sought to integrate existentialist themes with a feminist analysis of gender, highlighting the importance of considering women's lived experiences in philosophical discussions about existence and freedom.

Within the existentialist movement itself, there have been significant debates and misconceptions. One common misconception is that existentialism is inherently nihilistic and pessimistic. While existentialism does confront themes of meaninglessness and absurdity, it does not necessarily advocate for despair or nihilism. Figures like Camus and Frankl, for example, emphasize the potential for finding meaning and purpose even in the face of absurdity and suffering. Camus' concept of the "absurd hero" and Frankl's focus on the search for meaning in the midst of suffering both illustrate a more hopeful and resilient approach to existentialist themes.

Another internal debate within existentialism revolves around the role of the divine and religious faith. Kierkegaard, a deeply religious thinker, saw faith as a central aspect of human existence and argued that true meaning could only be found through a relationship with God. In contrast, atheistic existentialists like Sartre and Camus rejected the notion of a transcendent being and emphasized human freedom and responsibility in a godless universe. This debate highlights the diversity within existentialism and the different ways in which existential themes can be interpreted and applied.

The existentialist emphasis on individual freedom and authenticity has also been a point of contention. Critics argue that this focus can lead to a form of solipsism or moral relativism, where individuals are seen as the sole arbiters of meaning and value. This critique suggests that existentialism's rejection of objective moral standards and its emphasis on personal choice can undermine ethical responsibility and social cohesion. Existentialists, however, counter that the acknowledgment of freedom and the responsibility that comes with it can actually foster a deeper sense of ethical commitment and personal integrity.

In the 21st century, existentialism remains relevant but also faces new criticisms and challenges. One contemporary critique concerns existentialism's applicability in a multicultural and globalized world. Critics argue that existentialism, with its roots in European philosophy and its focus on individual experience, may not adequately address the diverse cultural contexts and collective dimensions of human existence. This critique calls for a more inclusive and cross-cultural approach to existential themes, one that considers the ways in which different cultural and social contexts shape existential concerns.

Another contemporary criticism of existentialism relates to the rise of technology and the digital age. Some critics argue that existentialism, with its emphasis on face-to-face human relationships and the authenticity of personal experience, may struggle to address the complexities of modern digital life. The pervasive influence of social media, virtual reality, and artificial intelligence presents new existential challenges, such as the nature of identity in digital spaces and the impact of technological mediation on human relationships. Existentialists are called to engage with these new realities and to explore how existential themes can be applied in a technologically saturated world.

Despite these criticisms, existentialism continues to offer valuable insights into the human condition. Its emphasis on personal freedom, authenticity, and the search for meaning resonates with many people facing existential crises and uncertainties in contemporary life. Existential themes are particularly relevant in the context of mental health and psychotherapy, where existential therapy provides a framework for addressing issues of meaning, purpose, and authenticity. The works of existential therapists like Viktor Frankl and Rollo May continue to influence contemporary therapeutic practices, highlighting the enduring relevance of existentialist ideas.

Existentialism also remains influential in the arts and literature. Contemporary writers and artists continue to explore existential themes, drawing on the rich tradition of existentialist thought to address questions of identity, freedom, and the human experience. The existentialist focus on subjective experience and the complexities of human existence provides a fertile ground for creative expression and artistic exploration.

In the realm of political and social thought, existentialism's emphasis on personal responsibility and ethical commitment has inspired movements for social justice and human rights. The existentialist call to live authentically and to confront the realities of oppression and injustice resonates with contemporary struggles for equality and human dignity. Existential themes can be seen in various social movements that advocate for personal and collective empowerment, challenging individuals to take responsibility for their actions and to work towards a more just and humane world.

In conclusion, existentialism has faced numerous critiques and controversies from various philosophical perspectives, including analytic philosophy, Marxism, and feminism. These critiques highlight fundamental disagreements about the nature of human existence, freedom, and the pursuit of meaning. Within the existentialist movement itself, there have been significant debates and misconceptions, particularly regarding the role of the divine and the potential for nihilism. In the 21st century, existentialism continues to be relevant but also encounters new criticisms in the context of multiculturalism, globalization, and technological advancement. Despite these challenges, existentialism remains a powerful and influential framework for understanding the human condition, offering valuable insights into the complexities of existence and the search for meaning and authenticity.

SECTION THREE: ANALYSIS OF NO EXIT

10. NO EXIT: A BRIEF SYNOPSIS OF SARTRE'S EXISTENTIAL PLAY

Jean-Paul Sartre, a towering figure in 20th-century philosophy, is renowned for his profound contributions to existentialist literature and thought. Among his many works, "No Exit" ("Huis Clos" in French), written in 1944, stands out as a quintessential existentialist play that encapsulates Sartre's views on human freedom, responsibility, and the nature of existence. The play's famous line, "Hell is other people," has become a key expression of existentialist thought, symbolizing the torment of being perpetually observed and judged by others. "No Exit" remains a significant work for its exploration of existential themes and its stark, minimalist portrayal of human interactions under extreme conditions.

The plot of "No Exit" unfolds in a single, unadorned room that serves as Sartre's vision of hell. This setting is crucial to the play's exploration of existentialist ideas, as it strips away external distractions and forces the characters—and the audience—to confront the raw dynamics of human relationships and self-perception. The room is furnished simply with Second Empire-style furniture: three sofas of different colors and a bronze mantelpiece. There are no mirrors, no windows, and the door is locked, creating a sense of claustrophobic entrapment.

The play introduces three main characters: Joseph Garcin, Inès Serrano, and Estelle Rigault. Each character arrives in the room believing they are alone in their torment, only to realize that they must share this eternal space with others. Garcin, a journalist and pacifist, is the first to arrive. He is soon joined by Inès, a manipulative and sadistic postal clerk, and finally by Estelle, a vain and superficial socialite. The Valet, a minor character who ushers them into the room, leaves them to their fate.

As the characters interact, they begin to reveal the reasons for their damnation. Garcin is tormented by his cowardice and betrayal, having fled to avoid persecution during a time of war and mistreated his wife. Inès, a self-proclaimed cruel and perceptive woman, is damned for manipulating a previous lover into murdering her husband, eventually leading to both their deaths. Estelle, outwardly innocent and coquettish, is revealed to have drowned her newborn child, an act that drove her lover to suicide. These confessions lay bare their moral failures and the choices that led them to hell.

The dynamics between the characters quickly become intense and confrontational. Garcin initially seeks validation from the women to assuage his guilt and affirm his bravery. Inès, on the other hand, relishes in psychological manipulation, understanding that their suffering is magnified by their interactions. She takes pleasure in tormenting Garcin and Estelle, knowing that her cruelty is a means of control. Estelle, desperate for male attention and incapable of accepting her own guilt, attempts to seduce Garcin to feel alive and desirable.

The realization of their situation dawns gradually. They come to understand that there is no physical torture in this version of hell—only the torment of each other's presence and their own unrelenting self-awareness. They are condemned to be each other's torturers, an insight that crystallizes in Garcin's famous line, "Hell is other people." This line encapsulates the existentialist view that much of human suffering arises from the gaze and judgment of others, which forces individuals to confront the parts of themselves they might prefer to ignore or deny.

As the play progresses, the characters' true natures are exposed. Garcin's repeated attempts to justify his actions and prove his courage are thwarted by Inès's relentless probing and Estelle's shallow affirmations. Inès, who seeks to dominate through her understanding of human nature, reveals her own vulnerabilities and the depth of her cruelty. Estelle, in her refusal to acknowledge her crimes, shows the emptiness of a life lived without introspection or moral consideration.

The climax of "No Exit" occurs when Garcin tries to escape through the door, which unexpectedly opens. However, he cannot bring himself to leave, realizing that he is bound not by physical constraints but by his need for validation from Inès. His inability to escape underscores the existentialist theme of self-imposed psychological and moral imprisonment. The door's opening and Garcin's subsequent decision to stay symbolize the existential belief that true freedom comes from within and is bound by our own choices and self-perceptions.

In the final moments of the play, the characters resign themselves to their eternal fate. They acknowledge that they are inextricably linked, each serving as a mirror to the others' flaws and failings. The play ends on a note of grim acceptance, with the characters sitting together in silence, aware that their torment is endless and self-inflicted.

"No Exit" has had a significant impact on existentialist thought and remains relevant in contemporary discussions of philosophy and human relationships. The play's exploration of the themes of freedom, responsibility, and the nature of existence provides a stark illustration of Sartre's philosophical ideas. The setting, a single room in hell, serves as a metaphor for the existential condition, where individuals are confronted with their own choices and the inescapable presence of others.

The idea that "hell is other people" highlights the existential belief that much of human suffering is rooted in the dynamics of social interactions and the judgments of others. This concept has resonated deeply with audiences, offering a powerful critique of the ways in which people seek validation and construct their identities through the eyes of others. It challenges individuals to consider the extent to which they are influenced by external perceptions and to confront the realities of their own existence.

Moreover, "No Exit" underscores the importance of authenticity and self-awareness in existentialist thought. The characters' inability to escape their own nature and the judgment of others illustrates the existentialist idea that true freedom and meaning can only be found through honest self-examination and acceptance of responsibility for one's actions. The play encourages viewers to reflect on their own lives and the ways in which they might be complicit in their own psychological and moral imprisonment.

In contemporary society, "No Exit" continues to be relevant as it addresses timeless questions about human existence, freedom, and the nature of relationships. The play's exploration of the psychological dynamics of entrapment and the search for validation resonates with modern audiences, who face similar challenges in navigating the complexities of social interactions and self-perception in an increasingly interconnected world.

The enduring relevance of "No Exit" is also evident in its influence on various forms of media and popular culture. The play's themes and central ideas have been referenced and adapted in numerous films, television shows, and literary works, attesting to its profound impact on how existentialist concepts are understood and represented. The minimalist setting and intense focus on character interactions make it a powerful piece for stage performances, continuing to captivate audiences with its raw and unflinching examination of the human condition.

In conclusion, "No Exit" by Jean-Paul Sartre is a seminal work in existentialist literature that offers a profound exploration of human freedom, responsibility, and the nature of existence. Through its stark setting and complex character dynamics, the play illustrates the existentialist belief that much of human suffering arises from the gaze and judgment of others. The idea that "hell is other people" encapsulates the challenges of living authentically in a world where social interactions and external perceptions play a significant role in shaping our identities. "No Exit" remains a powerful and relevant work that continues to inspire reflection and discussion on the fundamental questions of human existence, making it a cornerstone of existentialist thought and a timeless piece of literature.

11. EXPLORING THE DEPTHS: CHARACTERS AND THEMES IN NO EXIT

Jean-Paul Sartre's play "No Exit" is a cornerstone of existentialist literature, renowned for its intense character interactions and exploration of existential themes. The plot centers around three characters—Joseph Garcin, Inès Serrano, and Estelle Rigault—who find themselves trapped in a room together in hell. The room, furnished in the style of the French Second Empire, serves as the stage for their eternal torment. Unlike traditional depictions of hell, Sartre's version involves no physical torture; instead, the characters are subjected to the psychological anguish of being perpetually observed and judged by each other. As the play progresses, they come to realize that they are each other's torturers, embodying Sartre's famous line, "Hell is other people."

Joseph Garcin, a journalist and pacifist, is the first character introduced in the play. He arrives in the room escorted by a valet and is initially confused about his fate. Garcin's background reveals a man who prided himself on his intellectualism and moral superiority. However, beneath this facade lies a deep-seated cowardice. Garcin fled his country during a time of war, abandoning his colleagues and ultimately being executed by a firing squad. His primary struggle throughout the play is his desperate need for validation. Garcin seeks reassurance from the other characters that he is not a coward, attempting to construct a narrative in which his actions were justified and his moral integrity remains intact. This need for validation exposes his deep insecurity and his inability to confront the truth about himself.

Inès Serrano, the second character to arrive, is a postal clerk who is acutely aware of their situation from the outset. Unlike Garcin, Inès embraces her role as a torturer and manipulator. Her background is marked by cruelty and sadism; she seduced her cousin's wife, leading to the cousin's death and eventually causing her lover's suicide. Inès's personality is defined by her perceptiveness and her enjoyment in psychologically tormenting others. She quickly identifies Garcin's weaknesses and exploits them, asserting control over the dynamics in the room. Inès's awareness of their eternal punishment allows her to manipulate the others effectively, and she takes pleasure in the power she wields. Her character embodies the existentialist theme of bad faith, as she forces others to confront their self-deceptions while remaining brutally honest about her own nature.

Estelle Rigault, the final character to enter the room, is a wealthy socialite whose life revolved around vanity and superficiality. Estelle's background reveals a woman who sought validation through the adoration of men. She married for money and engaged in numerous affairs, the most significant of which resulted in the birth of a child whom she later drowned. Her lover's subsequent suicide adds to her guilt. Estelle's personality is characterized by her dependence on others for validation and her denial of her own moral failures. Throughout the play, she clings to her need for male attention, attempting to seduce Garcin to reaffirm her worth and distract herself from the reality of her actions. Estelle's vanity and refusal to acknowledge the truth about herself highlight the theme of self-deception and the lengths to which individuals will go to avoid facing their own guilt and shortcomings.

Sartre's depiction of hell in "No Exit" is a radical departure from traditional notions of physical torment. Instead, he presents hell as a state of perpetual psychological anguish, where the characters are condemned to eternal self-examination and judgment by others. The room itself, with its lack of mirrors and inability to escape, symbolizes the inescapable nature of their punishment. This setting forces the characters to confront their own identities and the consequences of their actions without any respite. The psychological torment is heightened by their interactions, as they become each other's mirrors, reflecting and magnifying their flaws and insecurities. Sartre's hell is a place where the characters are stripped of their illusions and forced to exist in a state of raw, unfiltered self-awareness.

A central theme in "No Exit" is self-deception. Each character enters the room with a carefully constructed narrative about their life and actions. Garcin deceives himself by trying to believe he was a principled pacifist rather than a coward who abandoned his comrades. Inès, while more honest about her cruelty, uses her awareness to manipulate and control, maintaining a facade of strength. Estelle's self-deception is perhaps the most pronounced, as she refuses to acknowledge her role in her lover's suicide and the drowning of her child. Throughout the play, the characters' interactions force these deceptions to unravel. The lack of mirrors in the room symbolizes their inability to see themselves clearly, both literally and metaphorically. Instead, they rely on each other's perceptions, which serve to strip away their illusions and expose their true selves.

Interpersonal conflict is a driving force in "No Exit," with the dynamics between Garcin, Inès, and Estelle forming the crux of the play's tension. Each character's flaws and insecurities are brought to the surface through their interactions. Garcin's need for validation makes him susceptible to Inès's manipulations, while Estelle's desperation for male attention creates a volatile triangle of desire and rejection. Inès's sadistic pleasure in tormenting the others adds to the conflict, as she actively seeks to disrupt any potential alliances and ensure their mutual suffering. The characters' inability to escape each other's presence and judgment leads to escalating tensions and a cycle of psychological torment.

This conflict illustrates Sartre's existentialist view that much of human suffering is rooted in the dynamics of social interactions and the constant need for validation from others.

The climax of the play occurs when Garcin attempts to escape through the door, which briefly opens. However, he ultimately cannot leave, as he realizes he is psychologically bound to the others' judgment. This moment underscores the existentialist idea that true freedom is internal and self-imposed, rather than determined by external circumstances. Garcin's decision to stay, despite the possibility of physical escape, highlights the inescapable nature of their psychological torment. The characters are trapped not by the room itself, but by their own need for validation and their inability to confront their true selves.

In the final moments of "No Exit," the characters reach a grim acceptance of their fate. They acknowledge that they are each other's torturers and that their torment is eternal. This conclusion reinforces the existentialist themes of freedom, responsibility, and the nature of human existence. The characters' eternal punishment is not a result of external forces, but of their own choices and the dynamics of their relationships. Sartre's play ultimately challenges viewers to reflect on their own lives and the ways in which they might be complicit in their psychological and moral imprisonment.

"No Exit" remains a powerful exploration of existential themes, offering a stark portrayal of the human condition and the complexities of self-deception, interpersonal conflict, and the search for meaning. Sartre's depiction of hell as a state of psychological torment, rather than physical suffering, provides a compelling metaphor for the existentialist view of human existence. The characters' struggles with their own identities and their relationships with others serve as a poignant reminder of the importance of authenticity and self-awareness in the quest for personal freedom and meaning.

The enduring relevance of "No Exit" is evident in its continued impact on literature, philosophy, and popular culture. The play's themes and character dynamics resonate with contemporary audiences, who face similar challenges in navigating the complexities of social interactions and self-perception in an increasingly interconnected world. Sartre's exploration of the human condition in "No Exit" offers valuable insights into the nature of existence and the importance of confronting one's own truths, making it a timeless and influential work in the canon of existentialist literature.

12: EXISTENTIALISM IN "NO EXIT": SARTRE'S PHILOSOPHICAL VISION

Existentialism is a philosophical movement that emphasizes individual freedom, choice, and responsibility, as well as the inherent meaninglessness of life. Jean-Paul Sartre, a leading figure in existentialist thought, has profoundly influenced how we understand human existence through his writings, particularly his plays and novels. One of his most significant contributions to existentialist literature is the play "No Exit," which encapsulates his philosophical vision. In "No Exit," Sartre explores key existential concepts such as the nature of hell, bad faith and self-deception, and human freedom and responsibility. Through the interactions of its characters, the play delves deeply into the existentialist themes of self-awareness, the gaze of the other, and the inescapable nature of personal responsibility.

The famous quote "Hell is other people" is perhaps the most well-known line from "No Exit" and one of the most frequently cited expressions of existentialist thought. This line encapsulates the essence of Sartre's view on human relationships and the nature of self-perception. In the context of the play, the quote is uttered by Garcin, one of the three main characters, as he realizes that the true torture of hell is not physical suffering but the perpetual scrutiny and judgment of others. This realization highlights Sartre's belief that our sense of self is significantly influenced by how others perceive us. The characters in "No Exit" become each other's torturers because they cannot escape the constant gaze and evaluation of the others, which forces them to confront their own flaws and moral failings.

The characters—Garcin, Inez, and Estelle—are condemned to an eternity together in a single room, each becoming a mirror reflecting the others' true selves. Garcin, a journalist who fled to avoid persecution and mistreated his wife, seeks validation and fears being labeled a coward. Inez, a manipulative and sadistic woman, relishes in the psychological torment she can inflict on the others, seeing through their self-deceptions. Estelle, a vain socialite, refuses to acknowledge her own guilt in causing the death of her child and her lover's suicide. Through their interactions, it becomes clear that they are each other's hell precisely because they strip away the comforting lies and self-deceptions that allowed them to avoid facing the truth about their actions during their lifetimes.

The concept of bad faith, or mauvaise foi, is central to Sartre's existentialist philosophy and is vividly illustrated in "No Exit." Bad faith involves self-deception, where individuals deceive themselves to avoid acknowledging uncomfortable truths about their existence. Garcin, Inez, and Estelle each exhibit bad faith in different ways, struggling to face their true selves and the reality of their actions. Garcin deceives himself into believing that his flight from danger was an act of principle rather than cowardice. He seeks reassurance from the others, particularly from Estelle, to validate his self-image as a brave and moral man. His inability to accept his own cowardice and the harm he caused his wife is a clear example of bad faith.

Inez, while more perceptive about the nature of their situation, also exhibits bad faith through her manipulation of others. She understands her role as a torturer and takes sadistic pleasure in exposing the others' weaknesses. However, this manipulation is also a form of self-deception, as it allows her to avoid confronting the deeper motivations behind her cruelty and her own insecurities. Estelle's bad faith is perhaps the most blatant. She refuses to acknowledge her guilt in her lover's suicide and the drowning of her child, instead clinging to her vanity and need for male attention. Her attempts to seduce Garcin and her constant need for validation are efforts to distract herself from the reality of her actions and maintain a facade of innocence.

The struggles of these characters to face their true selves and actions underscore the existentialist view that self-awareness and authenticity are crucial for living a meaningful life. Sartre believed that individuals often engage in bad faith to escape the anxiety and responsibility that come with true freedom. By deceiving themselves about their motives and actions, they avoid the burden of taking full responsibility for their lives. In "No Exit," the characters are forced into a situation where they can no longer escape this responsibility, and their bad faith is laid bare.

Sartre's view on human freedom and the weight of responsibility is another critical theme explored in "No Exit." According to Sartre, human beings are condemned to be free, meaning that they are always free to make choices and must bear the responsibility for those choices. This freedom is not liberating but burdensome because it requires individuals to confront the consequences of their actions and the reality that they alone are responsible for their lives. In "No Exit," the characters' past choices reflect their inability to accept this responsibility, and their eternal punishment is the inescapable confrontation with the consequences of their actions.

Garcin's attempt to flee from persecution and his mistreatment of his wife are examples of his refusal to take responsibility for his actions. He seeks validation from others to absolve himself of guilt, rather than accepting his own cowardice and the harm he caused. Inez's manipulation and sadism are ways of avoiding responsibility for her cruelty and the destructive impact of her actions on others. Estelle's denial of her guilt and her reliance on others for validation are attempts to escape the responsibility for her lover's suicide and her child's death.

The characters' inability to accept responsibility for their actions ultimately traps them in an eternal cycle of blame and denial. This reflects Sartre's existentialist belief that true freedom and meaning can only be achieved through the acceptance of responsibility for one's actions. By confronting the reality of their choices and their impact on others, individuals can achieve authenticity and live genuinely meaningful lives. However, the characters in "No Exit" are unable to reach this level of self-awareness and responsibility, and their eternal punishment is the endless confrontation with their own self-deceptions and the judgment of others.

In summary, "No Exit" is a powerful exploration of Sartre's existentialist philosophy, illustrating key concepts such as the nature of hell, bad faith, and the burden of freedom and responsibility. The play's setting and character dynamics provide a vivid depiction of how individuals create their own psychological torment through self-deception and the refusal to accept responsibility for their actions. The famous quote "Hell is other people" encapsulates the existentialist view that much of human suffering arises from the gaze and judgment of others, forcing individuals to confront uncomfortable truths about themselves. The characters' struggles with their true selves and their relationships with each other highlight the importance of authenticity and self-awareness in achieving a meaningful life.

The relevance of "No Exit" in contemporary discussions of existentialist themes is evident in its continued impact on literature, philosophy, and popular culture. The play's exploration of the human condition resonates with modern audiences who face similar challenges in navigating the complexities of social interactions and self-perception. Sartre's insights into the nature of human freedom, responsibility, and self-deception provide valuable perspectives for understanding the existential dilemmas of contemporary life.

For those interested in further exploring Sartre's existentialist philosophy, additional resources include his major philosophical works such as "Being and Nothingness," where he elaborates on the concepts of bad faith and human freedom, and "Existentialism is a Humanism," a more accessible introduction to his ideas. Additionally, reading other existentialist thinkers such as Simone de Beauvoir's "The Second Sex" and Albert Camus' "The Myth of Sisyphus" can provide a broader understanding of existentialist thought and its implications for human existence. These works offer profound insights into the complexities of living authentically and the ongoing search for meaning in a seemingly indifferent universe.

SECTION FOUR: ANALYSIS OF NAUSEA

13. NAUSEA: A BRIEF SYNOPSIS OF SARTRE'S EXISTENTIAL MASTERPIECE

Jean-Paul Sartre, a towering figure in existential philosophy, made a profound impact on literature with his novel "Nausea." Published in 1938, "Nausea" is considered one of the seminal works of existentialist literature. Through the experiences of its protagonist, Antoine Roquentin, Sartre explores themes of existential angst, the search for meaning, and the nature of human existence. The novel stands as a powerful representation of existentialist thought, providing readers with a deep and unsettling reflection on the human condition.

The novel is set in the fictional town of Bouville, a dreary and monotonous place that mirrors the existential malaise of its protagonist. Bouville is characterized by its grayness, routine, and the banality of everyday life, serving as the perfect backdrop for Roquentin's existential crisis. The town's name, which translates to "Mud Town," underscores the sense of stagnation and suffocation that permeates the narrative. Through his detailed and evocative descriptions of Bouville, Sartre creates an environment that feels both claustrophobic and inescapable, heightening the reader's immersion into Roquentin's inner turmoil.

Antoine Roquentin, the protagonist of "Nausea," is a solitary historian who has been living in Bouville for several years, working on a biography of an obscure historical figure, the Marquis de Rollebon. Roquentin's life is marked by isolation and a growing sense of disconnection from the world around him. He spends his days in cafes, libraries, and his small apartment, reflecting on his existence and the nature of reality. As the novel progresses, Roquentin begins to experience a profound and unsettling sensation that he describes as "nausea." This nausea is not merely a physical ailment but a deep existential realization of the absurdity and contingency of existence.

The novel unfolds through Roquentin's journal entries, providing an intimate and introspective look into his thoughts and experiences. Early in the narrative, Roquentin's nausea manifests as a vague and disconcerting feeling that he cannot quite understand or articulate. He becomes increasingly aware of the arbitrariness of the objects and people around him, feeling a growing sense of alienation and detachment. This sensation intensifies as Roquentin perceives the world as devoid of inherent meaning or purpose, leading him to question the very nature of existence.

One of the key plot points in "Nausea" is Roquentin's realization that his project on the Marquis de Rollebon is ultimately futile. He comes to see the biography as a means of avoiding his own existential crisis, a way to impose structure and meaning on a life that feels increasingly chaotic and meaningless. This realization leads Roquentin to abandon his work, further deepening his sense of nausea and existential despair. He is left with the stark recognition that he must confront the absurdity of existence without the comfort of external distractions or false purposes.

As Roquentin's nausea grows, he experiences a series of profound and transformative moments that lead to his existential realization. One such moment occurs during a visit to a local museum, where he is struck by the incongruity and absurdity of the historical artifacts on display. The objects, once imbued with significance and meaning, now appear to Roquentin as mere remnants of a forgotten past, devoid of any intrinsic value. This experience reinforces his sense of the contingency and arbitrariness of existence, heightening his existential angst.

Another pivotal moment in the novel occurs when Roquentin encounters an old acquaintance, the Self-Taught Man, in the local library. The Self-Taught Man is an autodidact who spends his days reading through the library's collection in alphabetical order, seeking knowledge and understanding. However, Roquentin sees the Self-Taught Man's pursuit as another form of bad faith, an attempt to impose order and meaning on an inherently meaningless world. This encounter serves as a stark contrast to Roquentin's own struggle with nausea, highlighting the different ways individuals cope with the existential dilemmas of freedom and meaning.

The climax of Roquentin's existential journey comes during a visit to a local cafe, where he experiences a profound epiphany. As he listens to a jazz song on the jukebox, Roquentin is overwhelmed by a sense of connection and transcendence. The music, with its spontaneous and improvisational nature, offers him a glimpse of a different kind of existence, one that embraces the fluidity and contingency of life rather than seeking to impose rigid structures and meanings. This moment of transcendence provides Roquentin with a sense of liberation from his existential nausea, allowing him to envision a new way of being that is authentic and free.

The novel concludes with Roquentin's decision to leave Bouville and abandon his former life. He resolves to write a novel that will capture the essence of his existential realization, a work that will embrace the contingency and absurdity of existence without seeking to impose false meanings or structures. This decision marks a significant turning point for Roquentin, as he embraces his freedom and responsibility to create his own essence through his actions and choices. The novel ends on a note of tentative hope, suggesting that while the existential struggle is ongoing, it is also a source of possibility and renewal.

"Nausea" has had a profound impact on existentialist thought and literature, cementing Sartre's reputation as one of the leading figures of existential philosophy. The novel's exploration of existential angst, freedom, and the search for meaning resonates deeply with readers, offering a powerful and unsettling reflection on the human condition. Sartre's use of the first-person narrative and his evocative descriptions of Roquentin's inner world create an intimate and immersive reading experience, allowing readers to engage directly with the protagonist's existential dilemmas.

The themes and ideas explored in "Nausea" have continued to influence existentialist literature and philosophy, inspiring subsequent generations of writers and thinkers. The novel's depiction of existential angst and the search for authenticity has been echoed in the works of authors such as Albert Camus, Samuel Beckett, and Iris Murdoch. "Nausea" remains a touchstone for discussions of existentialism, providing a rich and nuanced exploration of the challenges and possibilities of human existence.

In conclusion, "Nausea" is a seminal work in existentialist literature that offers a profound and unsettling reflection on the nature of existence, freedom, and meaning. Through the experiences of Antoine Roquentin, Sartre explores the existential dilemmas of alienation, bad faith, and the search for authenticity. The novel's impact on existentialist thought and literature is enduring, continuing to resonate with readers and inspire philosophical inquiry. "Nausea" stands as a testament to Sartre's genius and his ability to capture the complexities of the human condition in a compelling and evocative narrative. As such, it remains an essential work for anyone seeking to understand the depths of existential philosophy and the enduring relevance of Sartre's thought.

14. UNVEILING THE SELF: PROTAGONIST AND THEMES IN "NAUSEA"

Jean-Paul Sartre's novel "Nausea" is a profound exploration of existential themes through the eyes of its protagonist, Antoine Roquentin. The novel centers on Roquentin's experiences in the fictional town of Bouville, where he grapples with a profound sense of existential angst and the realization of life's inherent meaninglessness. Through his introspective journey, Roquentin undergoes a transformation in his understanding of himself and the world around him, ultimately confronting the absurdity and alienation that define human existence.

Antoine Roquentin, the central character of "Nausea," is a solitary historian working on a biography of an obscure historical figure, the Marquis de Rollebon. Roquentin's background and personality are marked by a deep introspection and a growing disillusionment with the world. His isolation is palpable, as he spends his days in cafes, libraries, and his small apartment, detached from meaningful human connections. Roquentin's personality is characterized by a sense of detachment and a relentless quest for understanding, which ultimately leads him into an existential crisis.

Roquentin's existential crisis is a central element of the novel. As he becomes increasingly aware of the arbitrariness of the world around him, he begins to experience a profound sense of "nausea" – a feeling of deep discomfort and disorientation that arises from his realization of the absurdity and contingency of existence. This nausea is not merely a physical sensation but a manifestation of Roquentin's existential angst. He perceives the objects and people around him as devoid of inherent meaning or purpose, leading him to question the very nature of reality and his place within it.

Roquentin's journey towards self-discovery is marked by a series of introspective reflections and transformative experiences. As he grapples with his existential nausea, he begins to see the futility of his work on the biography of the Marquis de Rollebon. This project, which he initially undertook to impose structure and meaning on his life, is revealed to be a distraction from his deeper existential concerns. Roquentin's decision to abandon his work signifies a turning point in his journey, as he confronts the need to find or create meaning in his own life rather than relying on external projects.

One of the dominant themes in "Nausea" is the sense of inherent meaninglessness that Roquentin perceives in the world. This theme is evident in his reflections on the objects and people around him, which he views as devoid of intrinsic value or significance. Roquentin's growing sense of meaninglessness is encapsulated in his observation that existence precedes essence – that is, things exist without any predetermined purpose or meaning, and it is up to individuals to create their own essence through their actions and choices. This realization leads Roquentin to a profound sense of disillusionment and despair, as he grapples with the weight of his own freedom and the responsibility to create meaning in an indifferent universe.

The theme of absurdity is closely linked to the sense of meaninglessness that pervades Roquentin's experiences. The absurdity of existence is a central tenet of existential philosophy, and it is vividly portrayed in "Nausea" through Roquentin's observations and reflections. He perceives the world as fundamentally absurd, with no inherent order or logic. This absurdity is evident in the arbitrary nature of objects and events, which Roquentin sees as disconnected from any larger purpose or meaning. His encounters with the banal and mundane aspects of life in Bouville further highlight the absurdity of existence, as he grapples with the realization that life is marked by contingency and unpredictability.

Roquentin's sense of alienation is another key theme in "Nausea." Throughout the novel, he experiences a profound detachment from society, others, and even himself. This alienation is evident in his interactions with the people around him, which are marked by a sense of disconnection and estrangement. Roquentin's relationships are superficial and unfulfilling, and he feels increasingly isolated from the world around him. This sense of alienation extends to his perception of his own identity, as he struggles to reconcile his inner experiences with the external reality.

Roquentin's detachment from society is mirrored in his physical and emotional isolation. He spends much of his time alone, reflecting on his existential concerns and the nature of reality. His solitary existence amplifies his sense of alienation, as he becomes increasingly disconnected from the social and communal aspects of life. This detachment is further compounded by his inability to find meaning or fulfillment in his work or relationships, leading him to question the value of human connections and the possibility of authentic existence.

Roquentin's alienation from others is also evident in his encounters with the Self-Taught Man, a character who represents a different approach to the search for meaning. The Self-Taught Man spends his days reading through the library's collection in alphabetical order, seeking knowledge and understanding. However, Roquentin sees the Self-Taught Man's pursuit as another form of bad faith, an attempt to impose order and meaning on an inherently meaningless world. This encounter highlights the different ways individuals cope with the existential dilemmas of freedom and meaning, and it reinforces Roquentin's sense of isolation and estrangement.

Roquentin's detachment from himself is perhaps the most profound aspect of his alienation. Throughout the novel, he struggles to reconcile his inner experiences with the external reality, leading to a sense of disintegration and fragmentation. This internal conflict is encapsulated in his experience of nausea, which signifies a deep discomfort with his own existence and the world around him. Roquentin's journey towards self-discovery involves confronting this alienation and seeking a way to integrate his inner experiences with his external reality.

The conclusion of "Nausea" marks a tentative resolution to Roquentin's existential crisis. As he listens to a jazz song in a local cafe, he experiences a moment of transcendence and connection that offers him a glimpse of a different kind of existence. The music, with its spontaneous and improvisational nature, represents a way of being that embraces the fluidity and contingency of life rather than seeking to impose rigid structures and meanings. This moment of transcendence provides Roquentin with a sense of liberation from his existential nausea, allowing him to envision a new way of being that is authentic and free.

In the final pages of the novel, Roquentin decides to leave Bouville and abandon his former life. He resolves to write a novel that will capture the essence of his existential realization, a work that will embrace the contingency and absurdity of existence without seeking to impose false meanings or structures. This decision marks a significant turning point for Roquentin, as he embraces his freedom and responsibility to create his own essence through his actions and choices. The novel ends on a note of tentative hope, suggesting that while the existential struggle is ongoing, it is also a source of possibility and renewal.

"Nausea" remains a seminal work in existentialist literature, offering a profound and unsettling reflection on the nature of existence, freedom, and meaning. Through the experiences of Antoine Roquentin, Sartre explores the existential dilemmas of alienation, absurdity, and the search for authenticity. The novel's impact on existentialist thought and literature is enduring, continuing to resonate with readers and inspire philosophical inquiry. "Nausea" stands as a testament to Sartre's genius and his ability to capture the complexities of the human condition in a compelling and evocative narrative. As such, it remains an essential work for anyone seeking to understand the depths of existential philosophy and the enduring relevance of Sartre's thought.

15. EXISTENTIALISM IN NAUSEA: SARTRE'S PHILOSOPHICAL INSIGHTS

Existentialism, a philosophical movement that emerged in the 20th century, places emphasis on individual existence, freedom, and the inherent meaninglessness of life. Jean-Paul Sartre, a leading figure in existential philosophy, contributed significantly to this field through his literary and philosophical works. One of his most impactful works, "Nausea," explores existential themes through the experiences of its protagonist, Antoine Roquentin. This novel serves as a vehicle for Sartre's philosophical insights, delving into the nature of existence, the rejection of essentialism, and the profound realization encapsulated in the concept of nausea.

At the heart of "Nausea" lies the concept of nausea itself, which serves as a metaphor for Roquentin's profound and unsettling realization of his own existence and the existential truths of the world around him. Nausea, in this context, is not merely a physical sensation but a deep existential awareness that strikes Roquentin as he perceives the arbitrary and contingent nature of reality. This sensation manifests in various forms throughout the novel, often triggered by mundane objects and situations. For example, Roquentin experiences nausea when he contemplates the existence of a tree root or the texture of a stone. These seemingly trivial encounters force him to confront the raw, unfiltered reality of existence, devoid of any imposed meaning or purpose.

The significance of nausea lies in its ability to strip away the comforting illusions and constructs that humans typically rely on to navigate their lives. For Roquentin, this leads to a profound sense of disorientation and discomfort, as he is confronted with the sheer contingency of existence. He realizes that objects and beings simply are, without any inherent reason or justification for their existence. This realization forces him to grapple with the absurdity of the world, as he comes to understand that there is no underlying essence or purpose that gives meaning to life.

This brings us to the exploration of contingency and the rejection of essentialism, which are central themes in "Nausea." Sartre posits that existence is contingent, meaning that everything that exists does so without any necessary reason or predetermined purpose. This stands in stark contrast to essentialism, the belief that things have a fixed essence or nature that defines their purpose and meaning. In "Nausea," Roquentin's existential journey is marked by his struggle to come to terms with this contingency. He realizes that his previous attempts to find meaning and order through his work on the biography of the Marquis de Rollebon are ultimately futile. The project, which he initially undertook to impose structure and significance on his life, is revealed to be a distraction from the deeper existential questions he faces.

Roquentin's struggle with the absence of essential meaning is a recurring theme throughout the novel. He perceives the world as fundamentally meaningless, with no inherent order or logic to guide his understanding. This realization leads to a sense of alienation and despair, as he grapples with the implications of living in a world devoid of intrinsic purpose. However, it also presents an opportunity for Roquentin to embrace his freedom and responsibility to create his own meaning. By rejecting the notion of a predefined essence, he is free to define himself and his existence through his actions and choices.

Sartre's existentialist principle that "existence precedes essence" is vividly embodied in Roquentin's experiences. This idea posits that individuals first exist without any inherent purpose or essence and only later define themselves through their actions and choices. Roquentin's journey in "Nausea" is a testament to this principle, as he comes to understand that he must create his own essence rather than rely on external constructs or predefined roles. His realization that his biography project is meaningless prompts him to seek authenticity and self-definition in other ways.

Roquentin's embodiment of the principle that existence precedes essence is evident in his evolving perspective on life and his role in it. As he grapples with his existential nausea and the recognition of contingency, he begins to see the possibility of living authentically by embracing his freedom and taking responsibility for his own existence. This shift in perspective is marked by moments of profound insight, such as his experience of transcendence while listening to a jazz song in a local cafe. The music, with its spontaneous and improvisational nature, represents a way of being that embraces the fluidity and unpredictability of life, offering Roquentin a glimpse of a more authentic and liberated existence.

In the final pages of "Nausea," Roquentin's decision to leave Bouville and embark on a new path signifies his acceptance of the existentialist principle that he must create his own meaning and essence. He resolves to write a novel that captures the essence of his existential realization, embracing the contingency and absurdity of existence without seeking to impose false meanings or structures. This decision marks a significant turning point for Roquentin, as he embraces his freedom and responsibility to define his own existence through his actions and choices.

In summary, "Nausea" serves as a powerful exploration of existentialist themes through the lens of Roquentin's experiences and realizations. The concept of nausea, as a profound awareness of the contingency and absurdity of existence, underscores the novel's exploration of key existential principles. Roquentin's struggle with meaninglessness and his journey towards self-discovery exemplify Sartre's ideas about the rejection of essentialism and the necessity of creating one's own essence. Through Roquentin's introspective journey, Sartre presents a compelling narrative that challenges readers to confront the fundamental questions of human existence and the nature of reality.

The insights presented in "Nausea" remain relevant in contemporary discussions of existentialist themes, as they address the enduring human concerns of freedom, meaning, and authenticity. Sartre's exploration of these themes continues to resonate with readers and thinkers, offering a rich and nuanced perspective on the existential dilemmas that define the human condition. For those seeking to delve deeper into Sartre's philosophical insights, "Nausea" serves as an essential starting point, providing a vivid and compelling depiction of existentialist thought in literary form.

For further reading on Sartre and existentialism, several resources can enhance one's understanding of these complex and profound themes. Sartre's own philosophical works, such as "Being and Nothingness" and "Existentialism is a Humanism," provide a more comprehensive exploration of his ideas and their theoretical foundations. Additionally, works by other existentialist thinkers, such as Albert Camus's "The Stranger" and "The Myth of Sisyphus," offer complementary perspectives on the themes of absurdity, freedom, and the search for meaning. These texts, along with scholarly analyses and critical interpretations of Sartre's work, provide valuable insights into the rich and multifaceted world of existential philosophy.

In conclusion, "Nausea" stands as a seminal work in existentialist literature, offering profound insights into the nature of existence, the rejection of essentialism, and the necessity of creating one's own meaning. Through the experiences of Antoine Roquentin, Sartre vividly illustrates the existential dilemmas that define the human condition, challenging readers to confront the fundamental questions of freedom, authenticity, and the search for meaning in an indifferent universe. Sartre's contributions to existential philosophy, as exemplified in "Nausea," continue to inspire and provoke thought, ensuring the enduring relevance of his work in contemporary philosophical discourse.

SECTION FIVE: COMPARATIVE ANALYSIS

16. COMMON THREADS: EXISTENTIAL THEMES IN NO EXIT AND NAUSEA

Jean-Paul Sartre, a central figure in existential philosophy, has profoundly shaped the field with his incisive explorations of human freedom, responsibility, and the inherent meaninglessness of existence. Two of his most influential works, "No Exit" and "Nausea," serve as foundational texts in existentialist literature, each offering a unique yet complementary perspective on the themes that define Sartre's philosophical outlook. Through these works, Sartre delves into the complexities of human existence, revealing the existential dilemmas that individuals face in their quest for meaning and authenticity.

"No Exit" and "Nausea" share several core existential themes, including the meaninglessness and absurdity of existence, self-deception and bad faith, alienation and isolation, and the profound implications of freedom and responsibility. These themes are intricately woven into the narratives and characterizations of both works, providing a rich tapestry for exploring Sartre's existentialist ideas.

One of the most prominent themes in both "No Exit" and "Nausea" is the inherent meaninglessness and absurdity of existence. Sartre portrays a world devoid of intrinsic meaning, where individuals must confront the stark reality that life lacks any predetermined purpose. In "Nausea," this theme is embodied in the experiences of Antoine Roquentin, who grapples with a profound sense of existential nausea as he becomes acutely aware of the arbitrary and contingent nature of existence. Roquentin's realization that objects and people simply are, without any inherent reason or justification, leads him to a deep existential crisis. This awareness strips away the comforting illusions of meaning, leaving him to confront the absurdity of life.

Similarly, in "No Exit," the characters are thrust into a situation that starkly reveals the absurdity of their existence. Trapped in a room together for eternity, they are forced to confront their own actions and the consequences of their choices without the possibility of escape or redemption. The play's famous line, "Hell is other people," encapsulates the existential absurdity of their situation, as the characters' interactions become a source of torment and self-realization. Sartre uses this setting to illustrate the arbitrary and often irrational nature of human relationships and the absence of any external meaning or purpose.

Another significant theme in both works is the concept of self-deception and bad faith. Sartre defines bad faith as the act of denying one's own freedom and responsibility by adopting false values or conforming to societal expectations. In "Nausea," Roquentin's journey is marked by his struggle to escape bad faith and confront the true nature of his existence. Initially, he immerses himself in the project of writing a biography of the Marquis de Rollebon, a task that provides him with a semblance of purpose and meaning. However, as he experiences moments of profound realization, he comes to see this project as a distraction from the deeper existential questions he faces. Roquentin's abandonment of his work signifies his rejection of bad faith and his embrace of the need to create his own essence.

In "No Exit," the characters are similarly ensnared by self-deception and bad faith. Each character enters the room with a carefully constructed facade, attempting to hide their true selves and the motivations behind their actions. As the play progresses, these facades are stripped away, revealing the characters' true natures and the extent to which they have deceived themselves. For example, Garcin initially presents himself as a courageous and principled man, but he is ultimately forced to confront his cowardice and the self-serving motivations behind his actions. The characters' inability to escape each other's gaze forces them to face their own self-deception and the inescapable reality of their freedom and responsibility.

Alienation and isolation are also central themes in both "Nausea" and "No Exit." Sartre portrays a world in which individuals are fundamentally isolated from one another, unable to truly understand or connect with others. In "Nausea," Roquentin experiences a profound sense of alienation from the people around him and from the world itself.

His interactions are marked by a sense of detachment and estrangement, as he perceives the inherent meaninglessness of existence. This alienation extends to his own identity, as he struggles to reconcile his inner experiences with the external reality.

In "No Exit," the characters' isolation is both physical and psychological. Trapped in a room together, they are unable to escape each other's presence, yet they remain fundamentally isolated in their own experiences and perceptions. The play's exploration of alienation is poignantly illustrated in the characters' interactions, as they attempt to manipulate and control each other while grappling with their own isolation. The inability to escape each other's gaze and the constant need for validation highlight the existential isolation that defines their existence.

The theme of freedom and responsibility is perhaps the most central to Sartre's existential philosophy, and it is vividly portrayed in both "No Exit" and "Nausea." Sartre posits that individuals are radically free to make their own choices, but with this freedom comes the burden of responsibility for those choices. In "Nausea," Roquentin's realization of his own freedom is accompanied by a profound sense of nausea, as he confronts the weight of his responsibility to create his own meaning. This awareness of freedom is both liberating and terrifying, as it places the onus of self-definition squarely on the individual.

In "No Exit," the characters are similarly confronted with the implications of their freedom and the inescapable responsibility for their actions. The room serves as a metaphorical space where they must face the consequences of their choices without the possibility of denial or escape. Garcin, Inez, and Estelle are forced to confront the reality that they are responsible for their own suffering and the suffering they have inflicted on others. This realization underscores the existentialist view that freedom is both a privilege and a burden, requiring individuals to take ownership of their actions and their existence.

In summary, "No Exit" and "Nausea" are foundational works in existentialist literature that explore the core themes of meaninglessness and absurdity, self-deception and bad faith, alienation and isolation, and freedom and responsibility. Through the experiences of their characters, Sartre vividly illustrates the existential dilemmas that define human existence. The themes presented in these works continue to resonate in contemporary discussions of existentialism, offering profound insights into the nature of existence and the human condition.

Sartre's exploration of these themes remains relevant today, as individuals continue to grapple with the search for meaning, the challenges of authenticity, and the implications of freedom and responsibility. "No Exit" and "Nausea" provide a rich framework for understanding these existential concerns, highlighting the complexities and nuances of human existence. For those seeking to delve deeper into existential philosophy, these works serve as essential texts, offering a compelling and thought-provoking examination of the fundamental questions that define our lives.

Further reading on Sartre and existentialism can enhance one's understanding of these themes and their broader implications. Sartre's philosophical works, such as "Being and Nothingness" and "Existentialism is a Humanism," provide a more comprehensive exploration of his ideas and their theoretical foundations. Additionally, works by other existentialist thinkers, such as Albert Camus's "The Stranger" and "The Myth of Sisyphus," offer complementary perspectives on the themes of absurdity, freedom, and the search for meaning. These texts, along with scholarly analyses and critical interpretations of Sartre's work, provide valuable insights into the rich and multifaceted world of existential philosophy.

In conclusion, "No Exit" and "Nausea" are seminal works that encapsulate Jean-Paul Sartre's existentialist philosophy, exploring the profound and often unsettling themes that define human existence. Through their vivid narratives and complex characterizations, these works challenge readers to confront the fundamental questions of meaning, freedom, and authenticity, offering a powerful and enduring reflection on the nature of existence. Sartre's contributions to existentialism continue to inspire and provoke thought, ensuring the enduring relevance of his work in contemporary philosophical discourse.

17. DIFFERENT PATHS: CONTRASTING EXISTENTIAL CRISES IN NO EXIT AND NAUSEA

In the world of existential literature, Jean-Paul Sartre's "No Exit" and "Nausea" stand out as seminal works that explore profound themes of meaninglessness, absurdity, freedom, and responsibility. While these works share common existential themes, they present contrasting approaches to the existential crises faced by their protagonists. The settings, character dynamics, expressions of existential angst, and resolutions in each work offer unique perspectives on Sartre's existentialist thought.

The settings and structures of "No Exit" and "Nausea" are starkly different, influencing the nature of the existential crises depicted in each work. "No Exit" is set in a single, confined room where three characters—Garcin, Inez, and Estelle—are condemned to spend eternity together. The claustrophobic setting emphasizes the inescapability of their situation and the intense scrutiny they face from each other. This enclosed environment creates a pressure cooker of psychological tension, where the characters' existential crises are magnified by their inability to escape or find solace in solitude.

In contrast, "Nausea" unfolds in the expansive, albeit mundane, town of Bouville. The novel follows Antoine Roquentin, who roams the town, grappling with his existential nausea. The setting allows for a more introspective and solitary journey, as Roquentin's crisis is deeply internal and personal. The expansiveness of Bouville contrasts with the confinement of the room in "No Exit," highlighting different dimensions of existential angst. While the characters in "No Exit" are trapped together, Roquentin in "Nausea" is free to move physically, yet remains trapped within his own mind.

Character dynamics play a crucial role in shaping the existential crises in both works. In "No Exit," the interactions between Garcin, Inez, and Estelle are central to the unfolding of their existential dilemmas. The characters are forced to confront their past actions and identities through the relentless gaze and judgments of the others. Garcin seeks validation of his courage, Inez desires to assert her power and manipulate others, and Estelle craves affirmation of her desirability. Their interactions create a dynamic of mutual torture, where each character becomes a mirror reflecting the others' insecurities and failures. This dynamic underscores Sartre's famous assertion that "hell is other people," as the characters' existential crises are exacerbated by their interpersonal relationships.

In "Nausea," Roquentin's existential crisis is more solitary. His interactions with other characters, such as the Self-Taught Man and his former lover Anny, are less central to his journey. Instead, his crisis is driven by his introspective reflections and encounters with the absurdity of existence. The characters in "Nausea" serve more as catalysts for Roquentin's realizations rather than active participants in his existential struggle. This difference in character dynamics highlights the contrast between external and internal sources of existential angst.

The expression of existential angst in "Nausea" and "No Exit" also differs significantly. In "Nausea," Roquentin experiences a physical and psychological sensation of nausea, which represents his profound realization of the contingency and meaninglessness of existence. This sensation is triggered by mundane objects and situations, such as a tree root or the texture of a stone, which force Roquentin to confront the raw, unfiltered reality of being. The nausea he feels is a visceral response to the absurdity of existence, stripping away the comforting illusions of meaning and purpose.

In "No Exit," the existential angst is expressed through the metaphor of hell. The characters' realization that they are condemned to spend eternity together, scrutinizing and judging each other, creates a psychological torment that represents their hellish existence. The absence of physical torture in favor of psychological suffering underscores Sartre's view of existential angst as an internal struggle. The characters' inability to escape each other's gaze forces them to confront their own failures and deceptions, making their existential crisis a communal experience.

The resolution, or lack thereof, of the existential crises in "No Exit" and "Nausea" further highlights the contrasting approaches of the two works. In "No Exit," the characters fail to resolve their crises. They are condemned to an eternal cycle of torment, unable to escape their self-deceptions and confront the reality of their existence. Garcin, Inez, and Estelle remain trapped in their bad faith, unable to achieve any form of authentic self-realization. The play ends with the characters resigned to their fate, underscoring the inescapability of their existential hell.

In "Nausea," Roquentin reaches a more tentative resolution. His decision to leave Bouville and abandon his work on the biography of the Marquis de Rollebon marks a turning point in his existential journey. Roquentin resolves to write a novel that embraces the contingency and absurdity of existence, seeking to create his own meaning rather than relying on external constructs. This resolution suggests a potential path towards authenticity and self-definition, even as it acknowledges the ongoing nature of the existential struggle. Unlike the characters in "No Exit," Roquentin takes a proactive step towards confronting his existential angst and embracing his freedom and responsibility.

In summary, "No Exit" and "Nausea" present contrasting existential crises that reflect different dimensions of Sartre's existentialist thought. The confined setting and intense character dynamics of "No Exit" emphasize the communal and interpersonal aspects of existential angst, highlighting the inescapability of self-deception and the torment of constant scrutiny. In contrast, the expansive and introspective journey of "Nausea" focuses on the solitary and internal nature of existential realization, exploring the visceral and psychological impact of confronting the absurdity of existence.

These contrasting approaches offer complementary perspectives on Sartre's existentialism, illustrating the multifaceted nature of existential crises. While "No Exit" emphasizes the relational and communal dimensions of existential angst, "Nausea" delves into the personal and introspective aspects of confronting the meaninglessness of existence. Together, these works provide a comprehensive exploration of the existential dilemmas that define human existence, offering profound insights into the nature of freedom, responsibility, and authenticity.

The implications of these contrasting elements for understanding Sartre's existentialist thought are significant. By presenting different paths through existential crises, Sartre highlights the complexity and diversity of human experience. The communal torment of "No Exit" and the solitary introspection of "Nausea" underscore the multifaceted nature of existential angst, revealing the various ways individuals grapple with the fundamental questions of existence. These works challenge readers to consider the interplay between personal and relational dimensions of existential crises, encouraging a deeper reflection on the nature of authenticity and self-definition.

For further exploration of these themes, readers may turn to Sartre's philosophical works, such as "Being and Nothingness" and "Existentialism is a Humanism," which provide a more comprehensive theoretical framework for his ideas. Additionally, examining the works of other existentialist thinkers, such as Albert Camus and Simone de Beauvoir, can offer complementary perspectives on the existential dilemmas explored in "No Exit" and "Nausea." These texts, along with scholarly analyses and critical interpretations, provide valuable insights into the rich and complex world of existential philosophy, enhancing our understanding of the profound questions that define human existence.

In conclusion, "No Exit" and "Nausea" offer contrasting yet complementary depictions of existential crises, reflecting the diverse dimensions of Sartre's existentialist thought. Through their vivid narratives and complex characterizations, these works illuminate the multifaceted nature of existential angst, freedom, and responsibility, challenging readers to confront the fundamental questions of meaning and authenticity. Sartre's contributions to existentialism continue to inspire and provoke thought, ensuring the enduring relevance of his work in contemporary philosophical discourse.

18. SHAPING THOUGHT: THE IMPACT OF NO EXIT AND NAUSEA ON EXISTENTIAL PHILOSOPHY

Existentialism, a philosophical movement that emerged prominently in the 20th century, addresses the fundamental questions of human existence, freedom, and the search for meaning in an indifferent universe. Jean-Paul Sartre, one of the leading figures of existentialism, significantly shaped the discourse with his literary and philosophical works. Among his most influential contributions are the plays "No Exit" and the novel "Nausea." These works not only lay the groundwork for existentialist concepts but also profoundly impacted philosophical discourse and continue to resonate in contemporary thought.

"No Exit" and "Nausea" are seminal works that establish key existentialist concepts such as freedom, bad faith, and the absurd. "No Exit," a one-act play first performed in 1944, encapsulates Sartre's ideas about human relationships and the nature of existence. The play is set in a single, confined room where three characters—Garcin, Inez, and

Estelle—are condemned to spend eternity together. This claustrophobic setting serves as a crucible for exploring Sartre's assertion that "hell is other people," highlighting the inescapable gaze and judgment of others as a source of existential torment. The characters' interactions reveal their attempts to escape the truth of their own freedom and responsibility, exemplifying the concept of bad faith. They deceive themselves about their past actions and motivations, seeking validation from each other while denying their own freedom to define their existence.

"Nausea," published in 1938, delves into the internal and solitary journey of its protagonist, Antoine Roquentin. Through his introspective reflections and encounters with the absurdity of existence, Roquentin grapples with a profound sense of existential nausea. This sensation arises from his realization of the contingent and meaningless nature of reality, forcing him to confront the absence of inherent purpose in the world. The novel vividly portrays the visceral and psychological impact of this realization, stripping away comforting illusions and revealing the raw, unfiltered reality of being. Roquentin's journey towards self-discovery and authenticity encapsulates Sartre's existentialist principle that existence precedes essence, emphasizing the individual's freedom and responsibility to create their own meaning.

The reception of "No Exit" and "Nausea" by contemporary audiences significantly influenced philosophical discourse and public understanding of existentialism. "Nausea" was Sartre's first major work of fiction, and it garnered significant attention for its innovative exploration of existential themes. Critics and readers were struck by the novel's unflinching portrayal of existential angst and the human condition, cementing Sartre's reputation as a leading existentialist thinker. The novel's impact extended beyond literary circles, influencing a generation of philosophers, writers, and artists grappling with the disorienting effects of modernity and the search for meaning.

"No Exit," with its compelling dramatic structure and penetrating dialogue, resonated deeply with audiences and critics alike. The play's exploration of human relationships and the existential implications of being observed and judged by others provided a powerful and accessible entry point into Sartre's philosophical ideas. Its success on the stage helped to popularize existentialism, bringing Sartre's concepts to a broader audience and sparking widespread interest in existentialist thought. The play's enduring popularity and frequent performances attest to its lasting influence and relevance.

The legacy of "No Exit" and "Nausea" extends beyond their initial reception, continuing to shape existentialist thought and contemporary philosophy. These works have become foundational texts in the study of existentialism, providing rich material for analysis and interpretation. Scholars and students alike turn to "No Exit" and "Nausea" to explore Sartre's ideas about freedom, bad faith, and the absurd, as well as to understand the broader implications of existentialist philosophy. The themes and concepts articulated in these works have influenced a wide range of disciplines, from literature and psychology to political theory and theology.

In contemporary philosophy, Sartre's exploration of freedom and responsibility remains particularly relevant. The emphasis on individual agency and the ethical implications of our choices resonates with ongoing debates about autonomy, moral responsibility, and the nature of selfhood. Sartre's insistence on confronting the truth of our own freedom and the need to create meaning in an indifferent universe challenges us to think critically about our lives and the values we espouse. "No Exit" and "Nausea" continue to inspire new generations of thinkers, encouraging them to grapple with the fundamental questions of existence and to seek authenticity in their own lives.

In addition to their impact on philosophy, "No Exit" and "Nausea" have left an indelible mark on literature and culture. Sartre's existential themes have influenced a wide range of writers and artists, from novelists and playwrights to filmmakers and musicians. The exploration of existential angst, freedom, and authenticity in literature and the arts reflects the enduring relevance of Sartre's ideas and their capacity to speak to the human condition. Works such as Albert Camus's "The Stranger," Samuel Beckett's "Waiting for Godot," and the films of Ingmar Bergman and Woody Allen all bear the imprint of Sartre's existentialism, illustrating the broad and lasting impact of his thought.

In conclusion, "No Exit" and "Nausea" are seminal works that have profoundly shaped existential philosophy and continue to resonate in contemporary thought. Through their vivid exploration of key existentialist concepts such as freedom, bad faith, and the absurd, these works lay the groundwork for understanding Sartre's philosophical vision. The reception and influence of "No Exit" and "Nausea" extend beyond their initial impact, continuing to inspire and challenge readers, scholars, and thinkers. The enduring legacy of Sartre's existentialist explorations underscores the importance of these works in the ongoing quest to understand the nature of human existence and the search for meaning in an indifferent universe.

The exploration of these themes in "No Exit" and "Nausea" provides a rich framework for understanding the complexities of Sartre's existentialist thought. By comparing the contrasting existential crises depicted in these works, we gain a deeper appreciation for the breadth and depth of Sartre's philosophy. The communal torment of "No Exit" and the solitary introspection of "Nausea" offer complementary perspectives on the existential dilemmas that define human existence, highlighting the multifaceted nature of freedom, responsibility, and authenticity.

For those seeking to delve deeper into Sartre's existentialism and its broader implications, several resources can enhance understanding. Sartre's own philosophical texts, such as "Being and Nothingness" and "Existentialism is a Humanism," provide comprehensive explorations of his ideas. Additionally, works by other existentialist thinkers, such as Albert Camus's "The Myth of Sisyphus" and Simone de Beauvoir's "The Ethics of Ambiguity," offer complementary perspectives on existentialist themes. Scholarly analyses and critical interpretations of Sartre's works also provide valuable insights into the rich and complex world of existential philosophy.

In conclusion, "No Exit" and "Nausea" are foundational texts that have significantly shaped existential philosophy and continue to resonate in contemporary thought. Through their exploration of key existentialist concepts and their vivid portrayal of existential crises, these works challenge us to confront the fundamental questions of existence and to seek authenticity in our own lives. The enduring legacy of Sartre's existentialist explorations underscores the importance of these works in the ongoing quest to understand the nature of human existence and the search for meaning in an indifferent universe. By engaging with "No Exit" and "Nausea," we gain a deeper appreciation for the complexities of Sartre's philosophy and the profound insights it offers into the human condition.

SECTION SIX: SARTRE'S PHILOSOPHICAL LEGACY

19. SHAPING MINDS: SARTRE'S INFLUENCE ON LITERATURE AND PHILOSOPHY

Jean-Paul Sartre, a pivotal figure in 20th-century existentialism, profoundly influenced both literature and philosophy with his extensive body of work. As a philosopher, playwright, novelist, and literary critic, Sartre explored the depths of human freedom, responsibility, and the search for meaning in an indifferent universe. His works, particularly "No Exit" and "Nausea," have left an indelible mark on the post-war literary scene and the development of existentialist thought.

Sartre's impact on post-war literature cannot be overstated. In the aftermath of World War II, writers and intellectuals were grappling with the profound disillusionment and existential crises brought about by the conflict. Sartre's existentialist themes of freedom, absurdity, and bad faith resonated deeply with this generation. His works provided a framework for exploring the human condition in a world that seemed devoid of inherent meaning or moral certainty.

"No Exit," Sartre's one-act play, was particularly influential in the theatrical world. Premiering in 1944, the play's depiction of three characters trapped in a room for eternity forced to confront their own flaws and the judgments of others struck a chord with audiences. Its famous line, "Hell is other people," encapsulated the existentialist idea that self-awareness and authenticity are often thwarted by the gaze and judgment of others. This play not only popularized existential themes in drama but also influenced the development of post-war theatrical traditions, contributing to the rise of the Theatre of the Absurd.

"Nausea," published in 1938, was Sartre's first major work of fiction and is considered a cornerstone of existential literature. Through the introspective journey of its protagonist, Antoine Roquentin, the novel delves into the existential realization of the absurdity and contingency of existence. "Nausea" vividly portrays the visceral experience of existential angst and the struggle to find or create meaning in a seemingly indifferent world. The novel's impact on existential literature was profound, influencing a generation of writers who sought to explore similar themes in their own works.

Several key literary figures were notably inspired by Sartre's ideas, helping to further disseminate existentialist themes in literature. Albert Camus, a close contemporary and sometimes rival of Sartre, explored existentialist and absurdist themes in his own works, such as "The Stranger" and "The Myth of Sisyphus." Although Camus and Sartre eventually parted ways philosophically, Camus's exploration of the absurd and the human condition paralleled and complemented Sartre's ideas.

Simone de Beauvoir, Sartre's lifelong companion and intellectual partner, also played a crucial role in the existentialist movement. Her groundbreaking work, "The Second Sex," expanded existentialist concepts to include a feminist perspective, examining the ways in which women's freedom and identity are constrained by societal structures. De Beauvoir's contributions helped to broaden the scope of existentialist thought, influencing both literature and feminist philosophy.

Samuel Beckett, another prominent figure influenced by Sartre, incorporated existentialist themes into his plays and novels. Beckett's works, such as "Waiting for Godot" and "Endgame," exemplify the Theatre of the Absurd, depicting characters in situations of waiting, stagnation, and existential uncertainty. Beckett's minimalist style and focus on the absurdity of human existence reflect Sartre's influence and the broader existentialist preoccupation with meaning and authenticity.

Sartre's impact on philosophy is equally significant. His role in popularizing existentialist philosophy cannot be overstated. Sartre's existentialism, which emphasized the individual's freedom and responsibility to create meaning in an indifferent universe, resonated with a post-war generation seeking to understand the complexities of human existence. His philosophical works, such as "Being and Nothingness" and "Existentialism is a Humanism," articulated the core tenets of existentialism and provided a comprehensive framework for understanding human freedom, bad faith, and the absurd.

Sartre's ideas were further expanded and interpreted by other philosophers, contributing to the development of existentialism as a major philosophical movement. Martin Heidegger's phenomenological approach and exploration of being heavily influenced Sartre's thought, and their intellectual exchange enriched both existential and phenomenological philosophy. Although Heidegger's and Sartre's philosophies diverged in significant ways, their contributions collectively shaped the existentialist discourse.

The critical reception of Sartre's works has been diverse and multifaceted. Philosophers and critics have both lauded and critiqued his ideas over time. Some have praised Sartre for his profound insights into human freedom and responsibility, while others have critiqued his existentialism as overly pessimistic or nihilistic. Despite these critiques, Sartre's works have remained a central focus of existentialist studies, and his influence continues to be felt in contemporary philosophical discourse.

The specific impact of "No Exit" and "Nausea" on existential philosophy and literature underscores their enduring significance. "No Exit" revolutionized theatrical traditions with its existential themes and innovative dramatic structure. The play's reception highlighted the resonance of Sartre's ideas with audiences grappling with the aftermath of war and the complexities of human relationships. Its influence extended beyond existentialist circles, shaping the development of modern drama and the Theatre of the Absurd.

"Nausea" similarly had a profound impact on existential literature. The novel's introspective and visceral portrayal of existential angst provided a template for exploring the absurdity and contingency of existence. "Nausea" has been instrumental in shaping existentialist thought, influencing subsequent literary works that grapple with similar themes of freedom, authenticity, and the search for meaning. The novel's legacy continues to be felt in contemporary literature, where existential themes remain a powerful lens for examining the human condition.

In conclusion, Jean-Paul Sartre's influence on literature and philosophy is both profound and enduring. His works, particularly "No Exit" and "Nausea," have shaped the post-war literary scene, popularized existentialist philosophy, and inspired generations of writers and thinkers. Sartre's exploration of existential themes—freedom, bad faith, the absurd, and the search for authenticity—resonated deeply with a world grappling with the disorienting effects of modernity and the quest for meaning. The legacy of Sartre's existentialist thought continues to inspire and challenge, ensuring his place as a central figure in both literature and philosophy.

For further exploration of Sartre's influence and existentialism, readers may turn to his philosophical texts, such as "Being and Nothingness" and "Existentialism is a Humanism," which provide a comprehensive understanding of his ideas. Additionally, examining the works of other existentialist thinkers, such as Albert Camus and Simone de Beauvoir, offers complementary perspectives on existential themes. Scholarly analyses and critical interpretations of Sartre's works also provide valuable insights into the rich and complex world of existential philosophy.

In understanding the impact of "No Exit" and "Nausea," one gains a deeper appreciation for the breadth and depth of Sartre's existentialist thought. These works not only encapsulate the core tenets of existentialism but also illustrate the diverse ways in which existential crises can be explored and understood. By engaging with Sartre's literature and philosophy, readers and thinkers are invited to confront the fundamental questions of existence, freedom, and authenticity, ensuring the continued relevance of Sartre's contributions to contemporary thought.

20. EXISTENTIALISM TODAY: THE MODERN RELEVANCE OF SARTRE'S IDEAS

Jean-Paul Sartre's existential philosophy, characterized by its emphasis on individual freedom, responsibility, and the inherent meaninglessness of life, remains profoundly relevant in contemporary society. His ideas continue to resonate in various aspects of modern life, from mental health and literature to film, art, and philosophical discourse. By examining how Sartre's existential themes are reflected in today's world, we can gain a deeper understanding of their enduring impact and significance.

In contemporary society, themes of meaninglessness, freedom, and responsibility are more pertinent than ever. The rapid pace of technological advancement, global interconnectedness, and shifting cultural norms have left many individuals grappling with existential questions about their place in the world and the meaning of their lives. Sartre's idea that "existence precedes essence"—that individuals must create their own meaning in an indifferent universe—resonates deeply in a time when traditional sources of meaning, such as religion and community, are increasingly questioned or fragmented.

The notion of freedom, a central tenet of Sartre's existentialism, is also highly relevant in modern life. Today's society offers unprecedented levels of personal freedom and choice, yet this freedom comes with the burden of responsibility. Sartre's exploration of "bad faith," the act of denying one's freedom and responsibility by conforming to societal expectations, speaks to contemporary struggles with authenticity and self-definition. The pressure to succeed, conform, and meet societal standards can lead to a sense of inauthenticity, where individuals feel disconnected from their true selves.

Sartre's existential ideas are particularly relevant in understanding and addressing modern mental health issues, such as anxiety and depression. Existential anxiety, the profound sense of unease that arises from confronting the fundamental uncertainties of existence, is a concept that resonates with many individuals today. The pressures and uncertainties of modern life can exacerbate feelings of anxiety and depression, leading to existential crises where individuals question the purpose and value of their lives. Sartre's emphasis on confronting these feelings and taking responsibility for one's own existence provides a framework for understanding and addressing these issues.

In the realm of modern literature, Sartre's existential themes continue to influence contemporary novels and stories. Many authors explore the complexities of human freedom, the search for meaning, and the struggles with authenticity in their works. For example, the novels of Haruki Murakami often delve into existential questions, blending surreal and introspective narratives that reflect the uncertainties and ambiguities of modern life. Similarly, the works of Ian McEwan frequently address themes of moral responsibility and the search for meaning in a seemingly indifferent world.

Film and television also reflect the enduring relevance of Sartre's existentialism. Many modern films and TV shows explore existential themes, portraying characters who grapple with issues of freedom, authenticity, and the absurdity of existence. For instance, the television series "Black Mirror" often examines the darker aspects of technological advancement and its impact on human identity and freedom, echoing Sartre's concerns about the loss of authenticity in modern society. Films such as "The Matrix" and "Eternal Sunshine of the Spotless Mind" delve into questions of reality, identity, and the nature of human existence, drawing on existential themes to create thought-provoking narratives.

Directors and screenwriters who draw on Sartre's ideas include Christopher Nolan, whose films such as "Inception" and "Memento" explore the nature of reality and the human mind, and Charlie Kaufman, known for his introspective and surreal narratives that question the nature of identity and existence. These filmmakers use existential themes to challenge audiences and provoke reflection on the deeper questions of life.

The influence of existentialism extends beyond literature and film into the realms of art and music. Modern art often grapples with themes of meaning, existence, and the human condition, reflecting Sartre's existential concerns. The abstract and often ambiguous nature of contemporary art mirrors the existentialist emphasis on individual interpretation and the search for meaning in an uncertain world. Artists such as Francis Bacon and Anselm Kiefer have created works that evoke existential angst and the struggle to find meaning amidst chaos and destruction.

In music, existential themes can be found in various genres, from rock and punk to electronic and experimental music. Bands like Radiohead and Nine Inch Nails explore themes of alienation, despair, and the search for meaning in their lyrics and compositions. These musical explorations resonate with Sartre's existentialist ideas, providing a soundtrack to the modern human experience.

Philosophically, existentialism continues to play a significant role in contemporary discourse. The existential emphasis on individual freedom, authenticity, and responsibility has influenced various philosophical movements and areas of study. For instance, existential themes are evident in feminist philosophy, where the focus on personal identity and the rejection of societal norms echo Sartre's ideas. Simone de Beauvoir's existential feminist work, "The Second Sex," remains a foundational text in feminist philosophy, exploring the ways in which women's freedom and identity are constrained by societal expectations.

Additionally, existentialism has influenced existential psychotherapy, a branch of therapy that focuses on helping individuals confront the fundamental questions of existence and find meaning in their lives. This therapeutic approach draws on Sartre's ideas to address issues such as anxiety, depression, and existential crises, providing a framework for individuals to explore their own freedom and responsibility in a supportive setting.

In conclusion, the modern relevance of Sartre's existential ideas is evident across various aspects of contemporary society. Themes of meaninglessness, freedom, and responsibility continue to resonate in today's world, influencing literature, film, art, music, and philosophy. Sartre's exploration of existential angst and the search for authenticity provides a valuable framework for understanding and addressing the complexities of modern life and mental health issues. By examining how Sartre's existential themes are reflected in contemporary culture, we can appreciate the enduring impact and significance of his philosophical contributions.

Understanding Sartre's legacy in both historical and modern contexts highlights the importance of his ideas in shaping contemporary thought and culture. His emphasis on individual freedom, authenticity, and responsibility continues to inspire and challenge us, encouraging deeper reflection on the fundamental questions of existence. As we navigate the complexities of modern life, Sartre's existentialism offers valuable insights and guidance, ensuring its continued relevance and influence.

For further exploration of Sartre's influence and existentialism, readers may turn to his philosophical texts, such as "Being and Nothingness" and "Existentialism is a Humanism," which provide a comprehensive understanding of his ideas. Additionally, examining the works of other existentialist thinkers, such as Albert Camus and Simone de Beauvoir, offers complementary perspectives on existential themes. Scholarly analyses and critical interpretations of Sartre's works also provide valuable insights into the rich and complex world of existential philosophy. By engaging with these resources, we can deepen our understanding of Sartre's contributions and their enduring impact on modern thought and culture.

21. BIBLIOGRAPHY

Primary Works by Jean-Paul Sartre

1. Sartre, Jean-Paul. No Exit and Three Other Plays. New York: Vintage Books, 1989.

- A collection that includes "No Exit," providing the primary text for analysis.

2. Sartre, Jean-Paul. Nausea. New York: New Directions, 1964.

- The primary text for "Nausea," essential for in-depth analysis of the novel.

Secondary Sources on Sartre and Existentialism

3. Aronson, Ronald. Jean-Paul Sartre: Philosophy in the World. London: Verso, 1980.

- A comprehensive study of Sartre's philosophy and its application to real-world issues.

4. Bakewell, Sarah. At the Existentialist Café: Freedom, Being, and Apricot Cocktails. New York: Other Press, 2016.

- An engaging introduction to existentialism and the lives of its key figures, including Sartre.

5. Catalano, Joseph S. A Commentary on Jean-Paul Sartre's Being and Nothingness. Chicago: University of Chicago Press, 1985.

- Detailed analysis of Sartre's major philosophical work, providing context for understanding his literature.

6. Flynn, Thomas R. Sartre: A Philosophical Biography. Cambridge: Cambridge University Press, 2014.

- An in-depth biography that connects Sartre's life events with his philosophical developments.

7. Murphy, Julien S. Feminist Interpretations of Jean-Paul Sartre. University Park: Pennsylvania State University Press, 1999.

- Examines Sartre's philosophy from a feminist perspective, providing a broader context for his works.

Critical Analyses and Interpretations

8. Barnes, Hazel E. Humanistic Existentialism: The Literature of Possibility. Lincoln: University of Nebraska Press, 1959.

- Explores existential themes in literature, including an analysis of Sartre's works.

9. Catalano, Joseph S. Reading Sartre: On Phenomenology and Existentialism. Cambridge: Cambridge University Press, 2010.

- A guide to understanding Sartre's complex ideas and their implications.

10. Howells, Christina. Sartre: The Necessity of Freedom. Cambridge: Cambridge University Press, 1988.

- Investigates the central role of freedom in Sartre's philosophy and its literary expressions.

11. McBride, William Leon. Sartre's Political Theory. Bloomington: Indiana University Press, 1991.

- Discusses the political dimensions of Sartre's thought, relevant for understanding his overall philosophy.

Additional Context and Philosophical Background

12. Heidegger, Martin. Being and Time. Translated by John Macquarrie and Edward Robinson. New York: Harper & Row, 1962.

- A foundational text in existential philosophy that influenced Sartre's thinking.

13. Kaufmann, Walter. Existentialism from Dostoevsky to Sartre. New York: Meridian Books, 1956.

- A compilation of key existential texts, providing broader context for Sartre's works.

14. Kierkegaard, Søren. The Sickness Unto Death. Translated by Howard V. Hong and Edna H. Hong. Princeton: Princeton University Press, 1980.

- An important precursor to existentialist thought, relevant for understanding existential themes.

Modern Interpretations and Applications

15. Camus, Albert. The Myth of Sisyphus. Translated by Justin O'Brien. New York: Vintage Books, 1955.

- Explores themes of absurdity and meaning, complementing Sartre's existentialist ideas.

16. Gordon, Lewis R. Existentialism and Social Engagement in the Twenty-First Century. New York: Rowman & Littlefield, 2016.

- Discusses the relevance of existentialism in contemporary social and political contexts.

17. Solomon, Robert C., and Kathleen M. Higgins. The Philosophy of (Erotic) Love. Lawrence: University Press of Kansas, 1991.

- Investigates existential themes in human relationships, relevant for analyzing Sartre's portrayal of interpersonal dynamics.

APPENDICES

1. TIMELINE OF SARTRE'S LIFE AND WORKS

Here is a comprehensive timeline of Jean-Paul Sartre's life and works, highlighting key events and milestones in his career and personal life:

1905

- June 21: Jean-Paul Charles Aymard Sartre is born in Paris, France.

1917

- Sartre's father dies, and he is raised by his mother and grandparents.

1924

- Enrolls at the École Normale Supérieure in Paris, where he meets Simone de Beauvoir, who becomes his lifelong companion and intellectual partner.

1929

- Receives his agrégation in philosophy, ranking first in his class. Simone de Beauvoir ranks second.

1931-1933

- Teaches at the Lycée du Havre and the Lycée de Laon.

1933-1934

- Studies in Berlin, Germany, where he is introduced to Edmund Husserl's phenomenology.

1938

- Publishes his first major philosophical novel, "Nausea" ("La Nausée"), which establishes his reputation as a leading existentialist thinker.

1939

- Publishes the short story collection "The Wall" ("Le Mur").

1940

- Is drafted into the French army during World War II and is captured by German forces, spending nine months as a prisoner of war.

1941

- Released from captivity and returns to Paris. Becomes involved in the French Resistance.

1943

- Publishes his philosophical magnum opus, "Being and Nothingness" ("L'Être et le Néant"), which outlines his existentialist philosophy.

- Publishes the play "The Flies" ("Les Mouches").

1944

- Publishes the play "No Exit" ("Huis Clos"), which popularizes the existentialist theme that "hell is other people."

1945

- Founds the political and literary journal "Les Temps Modernes" with Simone de Beauvoir and others.

- Delivers the lecture "Existentialism is a Humanism" ("L'existentialisme est un humanisme"), which becomes a popular introduction to existentialist thought.

1946

- Publishes the play "Dirty Hands" ("Les Mains Sales").

1947

- Publishes the essay collection "Situations I."

1948

- Publishes the play "The Respectful Prostitute" ("La Putain respectueuse").

1949

- Publishes the play "The Devil and the Good Lord" ("Le Diable et le bon Dieu").

1951

- Publishes the play "Nekrassov."

1952

- Breaks with Albert Camus over political differences.

1955

- Travels to the Soviet Union and China, reflecting his growing interest in Marxism.

1956

- Publishes "The Critique of Dialectical Reason" ("Critique de la raison dialectique"), combining existentialism with Marxism.

1960

- Publishes the second volume of "The Critique of Dialectical Reason."

1964

- Awarded the Nobel Prize in Literature but declines it, stating that a writer should not allow himself to be turned into an institution.

1969

- Publishes "The Words" ("Les Mots"), an autobiographical work.

1970

- Involved in various political movements, including student protests and Marxist causes.

1973

- Publishes "The Family Idiot" ("L'Idiot de la famille"), a study of Gustave Flaubert.

1974

- Suffers from health problems, including partial blindness.

1980

- April 15: Jean-Paul Sartre dies in Paris, France.

Posthumous Publications

- Various works, letters, and interviews continue to be published posthumously, contributing to the ongoing study and interpretation of his philosophy and literature.

2. GLOSSARY OF KEY EXISTENTIAL TERMS

Here is a glossary of key existential terms that are essential to understanding existential philosophy, particularly as articulated by Jean-Paul Sartre and other existentialist thinkers:

Absurdity

- The recognition that human efforts to find inherent meaning in life are ultimately futile in a universe that is indifferent or hostile to human concerns. This concept is central to existentialism and is vividly portrayed in the works of Albert Camus as well as Sartre.

Authenticity

- The idea of living in accordance with one's true self and values rather than conforming to external pressures or societal expectations. It involves acknowledging and embracing one's freedom and responsibility.

Bad Faith (Mauvaise Foi)

- The act of self-deception where individuals deny their freedom and responsibility by adopting false values or conforming to external pressures. This term is crucial in Sartre's existentialism, where bad faith is seen as a refusal to confront the truth of one's existence.

Being-for-itself (Être-pour-soi)

- A term used by Sartre to describe human consciousness, which is characterized by self-awareness and the ability to reflect on oneself. It contrasts with being-in-itself, as it represents a dynamic and fluid state of existence.

Being-in-itself (Être-en-soi)

- Refers to the existence of objects, which are fixed, complete, and lack consciousness. Unlike being-for-itself, being-in-itself is static and cannot reflect on its own existence.

Despair

- A feeling of hopelessness that arises from the realization that many aspects of life are beyond one's control. In existentialism, despair is often associated with the acknowledgment of one's limitations and the uncertainties of existence.

Existence Precedes Essence

- A fundamental tenet of existentialism that asserts that humans first exist without any predetermined nature or purpose and only later define themselves through their actions and choices. This contrasts with essentialist views that posit an inherent essence or purpose for human beings.

Facticity

- The aspects of existence that are given and cannot be changed, such as one's birth, past actions, and certain physical attributes. In existentialism, facticity is contrasted with transcendence, which represents the freedom to go beyond these given facts.

Freedom

- The existentialist belief that humans are free to make their own choices and define their own lives. This freedom is accompanied by the responsibility for the consequences of one's actions and the burden of self-determination.

Nausea

- A term popularized by Sartre's novel "Nausea," referring to the profound and unsettling realization of the contingency and absurdity of existence. It represents an existential awakening to the lack of inherent meaning in the world.

Nothingness (Néant)

- The concept that there is no inherent meaning or essence in the universe, and that individuals must create their own meaning through their actions. Nothingness also refers to the gaps or absences that define human consciousness and allow for freedom and creativity.

Other (Autrui)

- In existentialism, the Other represents other people whose existence and perceptions influence and define an individual's sense of self. The relationship with the Other is central to Sartre's idea that "hell is other people," as it involves the conflict between one's own freedom and the judgment of others.

Responsibility

- The recognition that individuals are accountable for their actions and the meanings they create in their lives. In existentialism, accepting responsibility is essential for living authentically and confronting the realities of one's freedom.

Transcendence

- The aspect of human existence that involves going beyond one's facticity and given circumstances. It represents the capacity to envision and strive for possibilities that are not determined by the past or external conditions.

Angst

- A deep, existential anxiety or dread that arises from the awareness of one's freedom and the responsibility to create meaning in an indifferent or absurd universe. This term is often associated with the existential crisis.

3. FURTHER READING AND RESOURCES

Here is a curated list of recommended books, articles, and media for further reading and exploration of Jean-Paul Sartre and existentialism:

Books by Jean-Paul Sartre

1. "Being and Nothingness" ("L'Être et le Néant")

- Sartre's magnum opus, a comprehensive exploration of his existentialist philosophy, focusing on concepts such as freedom, bad faith, and nothingness.

2. "Nausea" ("La Nausée")

- A novel that introduces existential themes through the introspective journey of Antoine Roquentin.

3. "Existentialism is a Humanism" ("L'existentialisme est un humanisme")

- A lecture that serves as an accessible introduction to Sartre's existentialist ideas.

4. "No Exit" ("Huis Clos")

- A one-act play illustrating existential themes through the interactions of three characters in a confined space.

5. "The Words" ("Les Mots")

- Sartre's autobiography, providing insight into his early life and intellectual development.

6. "Critique of Dialectical Reason" ("Critique de la raison dialectique")

- A work that integrates existentialism with Marxist theory, exploring the dynamics of history, society, and individual freedom.

Books by Other Existentialist Thinkers

1. "The Stranger" by Albert Camus

- A novel exploring themes of absurdity and the human condition through the life of an indifferent protagonist.

2. "The Myth of Sisyphus" by Albert Camus

- An essay that delves into the concept of the absurd and the search for meaning.

3. "The Second Sex" by Simone de Beauvoir

- A foundational feminist text that applies existentialist principles to the analysis of women's oppression.

4. "Man's Search for Meaning" by Viktor Frankl

- A memoir and psychological exploration of finding meaning in the face of suffering and existential despair.

5. "Fear and Trembling" by Søren Kierkegaard

- An exploration of faith and the individual's relationship with the divine, considered a precursor to existentialist thought.

6. "Being and Time" by Martin Heidegger

- A seminal work in phenomenology and existentialism, examining the nature of being.

Articles and Essays

1. "Existentialism and Human Emotions" by Jean-Paul Sartre

- A collection of essays that provide an accessible overview of Sartre's existentialist views.

2. "Camus and Sartre: The Story of a Friendship and the Quarrel that Ended It" by Ronald Aronson

- An analysis of the relationship and philosophical differences between Camus and Sartre.

3. "Existentialism as a Humanism" by Thomas Flynn

- An article providing context and analysis of Sartre's lecture and its impact on existential philosophy.

Online Resources and Media

1. Stanford Encyclopedia of Philosophy (SEP)

- [Jean-Paul Sartre](https://plato.stanford.edu/entries/sartre/)

- A comprehensive and scholarly overview of Sartre's life, works, and philosophical contributions.

- [Existentialism](https://plato.stanford.edu/entries/existentialism/)

- An in-depth entry on existentialism, covering its main themes and key figures.

2. Internet Encyclopedia of Philosophy (IEP)

- [Jean-Paul Sartre](https://iep.utm.edu/sartre-jp/)

- An accessible and detailed article on Sartre's philosophy and major works.

3. Podcasts and Lectures

- "The Partially Examined Life": Episodes on Sartre and existentialism, featuring discussions and analyses of his key works.

- "Philosophy Bites": Interviews with philosophers discussing existentialism and Sartre's contributions.

Films and Documentaries

1. "No Exit" (1954)

- A film adaptation of Sartre's play, exploring the existentialist themes of freedom and self-deception.

2. "Sartre by Himself" (1976)

- A documentary featuring interviews with Sartre, providing personal insights into his life and philosophy.

3. "The Road to Freedom" series

- A biographical series exploring the lives and philosophies of Sartre and de Beauvoir.

Contemporary Novels and Stories

1. "Never Let Me Go" by Kazuo Ishiguro

- A novel exploring themes of identity, freedom, and the human condition.

2. "The Road" by Cormac McCarthy

- A novel that delves into existential themes of survival, meaning, and human relationships in a post-apocalyptic world.

3. "Norwegian Wood" by Haruki Murakami

- A novel that addresses themes of memory, loss, and the search for meaning in modern life.